JIM HOHNBERGER

FACING FRENEMY FIRE

Pacific Press® Publishing Association
Nampa, Idaho
Oshawa, Ontario, Canada
www.pacificpress.com

Cover design/illustration by Mark Bond
Inside design by Steve Lanto

Library of Congress Cataloging-in-Publication Data

Hohnberger, Jim, 1948-
Facing frenemy fire : when friends attack—thrive, don't just survive /
Jim Hohnberger.
p. cm.
ISBN-13: 978-0-8163-2241-1 (hard cover)
ISBN-10: 0-8163-2241-4
1. Interpersonal conflict—Religious aspects—Christianity.
2. Interpersonal relations—Religious aspects—Christianity. I. Title.
BV4597.53.C58H64 2008
248.4—dc22
                                    2007027282

Additional copies of this book are available by calling toll-free 1-800-765-6955 or
by visiting http://www.adventistbookcenter.com.

08 09 10 11 • 5 4 3 2 1

Dedication

If you have been shot in the back . . .

If you are presently facing a firing squad . . .

If in the future you come under frenemy fire . . .

This book is dedicated to helping you find peace amidst your storm.

Acknowledgment

I want to express deep appreciation to my personal assistant, Jeanette Houghtelling, for her meticulous and steadfast labor of love as she edited, organized, and enhanced *Facing Frenemy Fire*. Jeanette, I couldn't have done it without you!

Table of Contents

Also by Jim Hohnberger

Escape to God

Empowered Living

It's About People

Come to the Quiet

Men of Power

A Note to the Reader

In this book, I recount certain incidents only to help the readers understand the conflict and its resolution—not to have them take sides or point fingers. Therefore, names have been withheld or changed in order to protect the privacy and identity of those involved. In every dispute, we would do well to pray for both sides, while encouraging all to find a fully surrendered experience in and through Jesus Christ.

Shot in the Back

Saturday, December 7, 2002, began balmy and beautiful at the Florida family camp meeting. My wife, Sally, and I chatted pleasantly over breakfast with the camp-meeting staff. Mark sat across the table from me and was in the middle of telling a humorous story when his cell phone rang. Reaching for his phone, he glanced at the caller ID as he tried to finish what he was saying. "Looks like it's for you, Jim," he noted as he handed me the phone.

"This is Jim," I answered, still chuckling over Mark's story.

My chuckle ended abruptly as the voice of Karl, my older brother, reached my ears. "Jim," he choked and paused for a moment as he groped for words. "Jim, Gary's dead."

"What! What happened? What do you mean? Are you sure?"

"Yes, I'm sure, Jim. Gary died in the night. His wife found him dead in bed this morning. We're not sure what happened. The coroner will be doing an autopsy to determine the cause of his death, but we suspect it was his heart."

My head started to spin. Breakfast no longer looked appetizing. Mark's story no longer seemed funny. The cheerful sounds of people visiting seemed terribly out of place. I had to get out of there. Stepping quickly out onto the porch, I leaned against the railing to steady myself as I continued to talk with Karl.

Gary, my youngest brother, was only in his midforties. He had suffered severe migraine headaches for years. Now he was dead—unexpectedly leaving his wife and children midstream in life. My tears flowed freely. Sally came to my side, concern written all over her face.

The look on my face and my rapid departure from the dining room had caught the attention of my ministry partners. They joined me outside. Hugging me, praying with me, they assured me that they were there for me. They would support me in whatever way I needed them.

I was scheduled to preach that morning. Could I? Should I? Or should I drop everything and fly to Wisconsin to be with my family? *Lord, what would You have me to do?*

At 11:00 A.M., I entered the pulpit knowing that, at that moment, my two brothers were delivering the alarming news to my fragile, aging mother. Would her heart bear the strain? Would she survive the shock? *Lord, I don't know how I can preach.*

"My grace is sufficient for you, Jim, for My strength is made perfect in weakness."

Before beginning my sermon, I shared with the congregation what was happening in my life and asked them to join me as I prayed for my two brothers and my mother. Then as I trusted myself with my God, He gave me special freedom to open my heart and plead with the congregation to recognize Him as real and present in their lives—and to give Him their undivided attention all day, every day. The people responded to God's Spirit and made heartfelt commitments.

Sunday morning, I preached the final message to close the camp meeting. At the end of the meeting, I invited all the ministry families and camp staff to join me on the platform to sing one last song together. Sally stepped to her usual place at my side, and my ministry partner came to my other side, putting his strong arm around my shoulders. We sang, "Family, we are family. Jesus, He is our God. And I'm so glad He brought us all together. I'm so glad that the Father is our God."

Monday morning found us still in Florida, visiting Sally's mother. Phone calls bounced back and forth between my brothers and me as we worked through the aftermath of Gary's death and made funeral arrangements.

In the midst of it all, my publisher called. "Jim, are you aware of a meeting that is being planned by individuals in your ministry?"

"Well, I know about our ministry work plans. What do you know that I don't?"

My publisher continued, "We've been asked to attend a meeting designed to prevent the publication of your upcoming book, *It's About People.*"

"What?" I replied. "Are you sure? Why?"

"Yes, I'm very sure, Jim. The purpose of the meeting is clear."

"Well, who's initiating the meeting?"

"As I said, individuals in your ministry."

A dagger entered my heart. It twisted and tore my heartstrings. "Who else is coming?"

"A church official and about four other individuals."

I paused, devastated. "So why are you calling me?"

"I'm calling you, Jim, because we have said we will attend only if you know about the meeting and are present as well."

"I wouldn't miss it. When is it scheduled?"

"December nineteen."

December nineteen—only ten days away! Was it really only yesterday that my friend stood with his arm around me singing "Family"? He must have known about the meeting then. Why didn't he talk to me? Why are my associates going behind my back? Why a clandestine meeting? What are they really up to? I don't believe it—it can't be! This isn't really happening! It must be a bad dream. I feel cornered. What will I do? How will I respond?

For days I pondered. I wrestled. I questioned. *Why? Why? Why? I don't understand. It hurts. It's betrayal. I trusted them. How could they do this? I feel like I've been shot in the back.*

And yet, during that time some things began to crystallize. For the first time, I could see a tangible tip of an iceberg I had sensed growing between us over a number of years—a cooling of the relationship, broken confidences, strange reports from mutual friends, the circulation of innuendos and half-truths, the inability to resolve relatively minor issues. These things had troubled me deeply. However, when I repeatedly approached my ministry associates, they denied all that I had sensed. I was too sensitive, they said. I needed just to trust their good intentions and put the best construction possible on their actions.

A term that my son Matthew had used began to echo in my mind—*frenemy.* A frenemy is someone who acts like a friend to your face but undermines you behind your back.

Friendly fire

The United States military calls it *friendly fire*—an attack by friendly or allied forces. Friendly fire is contrasted with fire originating from enemy forces. Some prefer the term *fratricide* over *friendly fire* because really there's nothing friendly about getting shot by your own side.[1]

Friendly fire incidents fall roughly into two categories.[2] The first classification is *fog of war,* which generically describes friendly fire incidents in unintentional circumstances. Fire aimed at enemy forces accidentally ends up hitting one's own soldiers, or friendly troops are mistakenly attacked in the belief that they are the enemy.

The second classification is *fragging*—essentially murder—in which friendly fire incidents are premeditated. This term came into use during the Vietnam War from the practice of assassinating an unpopular member, usually an officer, of one's own fighting unit by dropping a fragmentation grenade into the victim's tent at night. A fragging victim could also be killed by intentional friendly fire during combat. In either case, the death would be blamed on the enemy and, due to the dead man's unpopularity, no one would contradict the cover story.

Fragging was surprisingly common in Vietnam. At least six hundred American officers were murdered by their own troops in documented cases, and as many as fourteen hundred other officers' deaths could not be explained.[3] Incidents of fragging have been recorded in the U.S. military as far back as the American Civil War.

Friendly fire—wounded and sometimes killed by those we eat with, sleep with, train with, play with, and grow up with. But that's in war—certainly not in the church. Or is it? Where does war begin? Truly, the seed of all war is in the heart of an individual. When I choose of my own free moral agency to be *in charge* and to reject God's will and way, then the war of all wars begins—that is, who is going to rule in my heart

---

1. Geoffrey Regan, *Backfire: A History of Friendly Fire From Ancient Warfare to the Present Day* (London: Robson Books, 2002).
2. Ibid.
3. Geoffrey Regan, *More Military Blunders* (London: Carlton Books, 2004).

over this matter? Whenever I choose to be *the one in charge,* there are going to be casualties.

First casualty

The very first casualty of frenemy fire was God! That's right—the first fragging incident ever recorded took place in heaven, and the target was God Himself. And the aftermath is a war that involves you and me.[4] How did it begin?

It began with Lucifer, " ' " 'the model of perfection, full of wisdom and perfect in beauty . . . anointed as a guardian cherub . . . on the holy mount of God.' " ' "[5] He was called the "son of the morning."[6] He lived in a perfect environment, had a sinless nature, and occupied the highest position in the universe under God. Somehow, unexplainably, he became discontent. He wanted God's position. He wanted to be in charge. He boasted in his heart, "I will ascend into heaven, I will exalt my throne . . . I will sit also upon the mount of the congregation, . . . I will ascend above the heights of the clouds; I will be like the most High."[7]

Ohhh—ouch! There it is. Pride. Jealousy. Self-importance. Self-exaltation. Wanting more power, more influence, he *sold out* his Maker. Oh, it wasn't a frontal attack. No, he maintained the appearance of loyalty and fidelity. But behind the scenes, as he went about his duties, he dropped mild innuendos and inserted little slights. As time went on and his credibility grew, he began to spread slander, to create doubts and suspicion. Then finally he twisted and distorted the truth about God.

His plans were so skillfully laid and his tactics so subtly carried out that he convinced a third of the angelic host to side with his cause.[8] Did you catch that? Lucifer convinced pure and holy angels in a pure and holy heaven who lived face to face with a pure and holy God to rise up against their Creator. "War broke out in heaven."[9] Thus began the first

---

4. See Revelation 12:7–9.
5. Ezekiel 28:11–14, NIV.
6. Isaiah 14:12.
7. Isaiah 14:13, 14.
8. See Revelation 12:4.
9. Revelation 12:7, NKJV.

frenemy fire—God's character being the first target, and self-rule the hoped-for prize.

First family infected

This spirit of domination found its way into the first family. This conflict would not be behind-the-scenes guerilla warfare but an out-and-out attack.

Cain picked up the strain of Lucifer's song.[10] "I will be in charge. I will do things my way. God must submit to me. It's just a little thing—the fruit of my own labor instead of a lamb." But when he saw that his offering was not accepted while Abel's was, Cain became very angry—unreasonably angry. His countenance fell as jealousy, envy, and wounded pride surged through his being. Instead of surrendering these emotions to God and relinquishing his alliance with Lucifer's spirit, he allowed them to grow into a burning desire to dominate, to compel, to force.

In that spirit, Cain *talked* with Abel, his brother. Can you picture it? How do people talk when they are consumed with anger and wounded pride? They debate. They intimidate. They argue. They are forceful, compelling, controlling. Have you done this? Have others done this to you?

When Cain saw that he could not dominate and control Abel, he was so enraged that he took his brother's life. He shed his brother's blood because Abel worshiped differently, believed differently, talked differently—and wouldn't submit to the control of one who wanted to usurp God's position in his life.

God banished Cain from his family and placed a mark upon him. I believe that the mark of Cain is not extinct today. God sees that mark on every person who indulges Cain's spirit. Have you seen it? Do you bear it? Examine your own experience. I hardly know a family that doesn't suffer from some form of this bloodshed. When someone steps outside of others' expectations, mores, norms, cultures, or traditions, more often than not, someone's blood gets shed. Perhaps, not literally or mortally. But the wounds inflicted are nonetheless real and destructive. I experienced this frenemy fire when I changed from being a

---

10. Find the story in Genesis 4:3–15.

Catholic to being a Protestant. It touched off a firing squad that went on for years.

Oh, the horror of it! Can you imagine the agony of Adam and Eve? Their first two sons, both lost because of frenemy fire—one the assailant, the other the victim. Taken out by your own brother. Oh, the heartache of our first parents! Oh, the heartache of you and me!

Can't buy or sell

Unfortunately, the frenemy fire saga does not end with Genesis 4. You can trace it all the way through the story of the Scriptures and on down through the Christian era to the present. It has infected families, friendships, kingdoms, and churches. The book of Revelation prophetically picked up the strain of infection that characterizes the times you and I are now facing. The mark of Cain has not disappeared. Instead, it has swelled and rooted itself in the religion of the last days and will reach its culmination in the mark of the beast.

Read about it in Revelation 13. The beast wants to be in charge—in place of God.[11]

He makes war.[12] He dominates. He compels. He gains control through deception.[13] He requires submission. He demands worship.[14] If you don't do it his way, you will be economically boycotted.[15] And if that fails to bring you to submission, he will kill you.[16] His mark reeks with force, compulsion, control, and domination.

Contrast the attitude of the beast with the spirit of the Lamb of Revelation 5 and 14. The Lamb offers Himself. He is slain for us. He wins trust through demonstration. He redeems from bondage. He invites worship.[17] "Where the spirit of the Lord is, there is liberty."[18]

The hallmark of God's nature is liberty. The stamp of Lucifer's character is domination. These motivations are being revealed in their

---

11. See Revelation 13:4–6.
12. See verse 7.
13. See verse 14.
14. See verses 4, 8, 12.
15. See verses 16, 17.
16. See verse 15.
17. See Revelation 5:6–14; 14:1–12.
18. 2 Corinthians 3:17.

respective followers. And you can't tell who's who by their uniforms—by their profession. Lucifer, Cain, and the beast all wore religious garb and went through religious routines. But Christ's litmus test never fails: "By their fruits ye shall know them."[19]

So what does your fruit taste like when someone disagrees with you—thinks differently, worships differently, lives differently? Do you tinker, meddle, and prescribe? Do you play the role of "Junior Holy Spirit"? Do you give them the cold shoulder, drop innuendos behind their back, or spread gossip to tarnish their reputation? Do you twist the truth to your benefit? Do you manipulate, intimidate, coerce, force, or control? If you do, you are in the ranks of Lucifer, Cain, and the beast power—regardless of all your religious qualifications. That ought to be enough to wake us up! That kind of fruit never benefited anyone!

A king and a shepherd

Saul was a promising young man with almost unlimited opportunity. Tall and talented, he was also humble and teachable. He was little in his own sight.[20] God handpicked him out of thousands of other young men in Judah to be the first king of Israel. He flourished—at first. Then a familiar pattern appeared.

Saul found himself facing a huge Philistine force of "thirty thousand chariots, six thousand horsemen, and people as the sand which is on the sea shore."[21] Saul's soldiers examined the odds, and many concluded that desertion was the best option. The Israelite army rapidly dwindled to six hundred footmen. To make matters worse, the Philistines had made sure that no Israelite blacksmiths were open for business. Consequently, the only armed Israelites were King Saul and his son Jonathan. Would you find that situation stressful? I would, and Saul certainly did. His only hope for help was God! He had received strict instructions to wait for the prophet Samuel to arrive to offer a sacrifice and tell him how to proceed. But Samuel was a bit late. Saul started to get agitated, worried, and discontented. If he waited around

---

19. Matthew 7:20.
20. See 1 Samuel 15:17.
21. 1 Samuel 13:5.

much longer, he would have no army at all. He finally decided to be the one in charge. He took over and offered the sacrifice.[22] God appealed to Saul to acknowledge the path that he was on and turn around, but Saul persisted.

Jonathan, through a daring act of faith, almost single-handedly routed the Philistine forces. It was obvious that God had bypassed Saul and used someone who was willing to let God be God to save His people from their tormenters. The rebuke to Saul had to be obvious. But he didn't like that. He would not humble himself. Needing to save face, he made a rash oath saying, " 'Cursed is the man who eats any food until evening, before I have taken vengeance on my enemies.' "[23] Jonathan wasn't present when Saul said that—he was busy fighting the Philistines. Sometime during the day, Jonathan innocently tasted a little honey that he found in the woods to bolster his energy. When Saul found out, he ordered Jonathan's execution and would have carried it out if the army had not come to Jonathan's defense.[24] You see, whenever self-exaltation becomes the driving motivation, anyone who stands in the way is regarded as an obstacle to be mowed down—even a member of your own family.

The next episode in Saul's life was an encounter with the Philistine giant, Goliath. And that's when an obscure lad from a distant village entered the scene and became the obsession of the king. The little shepherd boy, David, was willing to do something the king was not—let God be in charge and trust utterly in His direction. Consequently, he accomplished what all the armies of Israel had failed to do. Goliath was beheaded, and the Philistines fled with their tails between their legs.

Saul was grateful. So far, so good. David was a nobody who made Saul look like a winner. David could be useful. So Saul hired David to lead a regiment of Israelites in a series of battles to further push back the Philistine incursion. David was overwhelmingly successful, and his popularity soared. As David was returning from battle one day, the women of the city danced out to meet him, singing, "Saul hath slain his thousands, and David his ten thousands."[25]

22. See 1 Samuel 13.
23. 1 Samuel 14:24, NKJV.
24. See 1 Samuel 14:1–46.
25. 1 Samuel 18:7.

This would be Saul's greatest test—and he failed, miserably failed. Jealousy, envy, and pride blinded Saul. He followed the pattern and found himself compelled to play something like the old game of Monopoly. Saul was driven to monopolize all the honor and glory and praise for himself. Hence, he could see this measly little shepherd boy as nothing but an obstacle to his own greatness. He *must* take David out regardless of what that required. It seems Saul had a touch of "Luciferitis." His pretend friendship grew into a nationwide manhunt for David's head. Saul was determined to frag David.

David, the little shepherd boy who desired only to honor God, found he had more to fear from his own people, his own leader, and his own church than he ever had to fear from the lion, the bear, and the Philistine giant. Once again, the deadly contest of frenemy fire began.

Listen to the agony of David's heart. "For it was not an enemy that reproached me; then I could have borne it: neither was it he that hated me that did magnify himself against me; then I would have hid myself from him: But it was thou, a man of mine equal, my guide, and mine acquaintance. We took sweet counsel together, and walked to the house of God in company."[26]

One of the deepest hurts is betrayal by a seemingly spiritual companion. Is that you? Look deep, friends, look very deep to see if any Luciferitis is in your tongue, your actions, or your motives. It's deadly stuff, and in the end it destroys the perpetrator more than the victim.

Just ask Cain, ask Saul, and by all means, ask Judas.

God's denominated church

Judas, too, followed the pattern of Luciferitis and bore the mark of Cain—discontent, a determination to be in charge, escalating pride, jealousy, covetousness, finally breaking out in premeditated frenemy fire. Even Jesus faced frenemy fire from within His own ministry. Given His decision to allow free choice, even God couldn't avoid it; Jesus couldn't avoid it and neither will you or I. We all seem to be tested by it—whether it's within our families, friendships, employment, neighborhoods, or churches. Somehow, someway, frenemy fire seems to show its ugly head.

---

26. Psalm 55:12–14.

Yes, it was frenemy fire that took Jesus out—not the Romans. Never was anyone more humiliated, heartbroken, insulted, tormented, and condemned than Jesus—by His own people. One in His closest ranks betrayed Him to those in His own church who hated Him! And together they sought to take out the One they thought stood in the way of their program.

The leadership of God's denominated church was jealous of Jesus' influence with the people and determined " 'that it is expedient for *us* that one man should die for the people, and not that the whole nation should perish.' "[27]

"Expedient for us." The dictionary defines *expedient* as "something done or a method used to achieve an aim quickly, regardless of whether it is fair, right, or wise in the long term."[28] That's the issue! What is best for Lucifer? What is best for Cain? What is best for Saul? What is best for the system? Not, What is right? What is principled? What is best for the other person? The justification for frenemy fire is what is "expedient for us."

Rubbed out by the religionists

Frenemy fire did not cease with the crucifixion of Christ. Still sparked by Lucifer, its casualties only mounted. The resurrected Christ was beyond Satan's reach, but Satan could still target Christ's ambassadors. "Rubbed out by the religionists" could be written on the tombstones of many of the early followers of Christ. Peter was threatened, imprisoned, sentenced to execution, and finally crucified upside down. James was executed publicly as an example of what would happen to those who should openly profess Christ. John was thrown into a caldron of boiling oil for believing differently from the establishment, and when God miraculously saved him from an oily death, he was exiled to a lonely work camp. Paul relates story after story of false accusations, deception, being hunted, stoned, beaten, imprisoned, and condemned to death. Do you see the thread of *control* running through all these stories? It's the mark of Cain.

27. John 11:50, NKJV, emphasis supplied.

28. *Encarta® World English Dictionary*, s.v. "Expedient," http://encarta.msn.com/dictionary_/expedient.html.

That thread continues to weave through postbiblical history. As the early church grew in numbers and popularity, the familiar pattern we've traced with individuals manifested itself in the larger body. Becoming discontent with the humble simplicity of Christ and the plain requirements of God, church leaders thought they could improve on God. They decided to be *in charge*. A spirit of compromise and conformity generated a host of human theories and traditions. And what is the next step in this progression? To obliterate every obstacle to self-exaltation. As the heavenly spirit weakens, the lust of dominion grows strong.

This lust of dominion indulged by "Christians" targeted the Huguenots and Waldenses for extinction. It fired the Crusades to the Holy Land. It lit the fires for unnamed legions of martyrs. It dogged the steps of all who uplifted the pure principles of God—Huss and Jerome, John Wycliffe, William Tyndale, Martin Luther, and many others. It tore apart the tenderest of human ties and shredded the consciences and bodies of men. And frenemy fire burns on, sometimes underground in subtle, alluring terms; sometimes overtly in all-out war. But the casualties continue to mount.

According to *The American War Library,* the incidence of friendly fire casualties is not decreasing with time.[29] The percentage of U.S. military casualties (both fatal and nonfatal) that resulted from friendly fire in World War II was 21 percent. The statistics from the Korean War were 18 percent, rising to 39 percent in the Vietnam War and 52 percent in the Persian Gulf War.[30] That is not a comforting trend.

Is it any better in the modern church? Of course, we don't burn people at the stake nowadays, but is "the lust for dominion" that sparks frenemy fire quenched? Are we content? Who is the one in charge in our lives? Is it God? Or is it us? Do we allow the desire for self-promotion to blind our eyes to the real enemy while we take potshots at our brother?

According to a survey conducted in the spring of 2004, 95 percent of 506 pastors had experienced church conflict, and one-fourth of them

---

29. The Michael Eugene Mullen American Friendly-Fire Notebook, "The American War Friendly-Fire Notebook," http://members.aol.com/amerwar/ff/ff.htm.

30. These statistics do not include murders or suicides.

were right then in the midst of the storm. The study indicated that 85 percent of all church conflict involves control issues.[31] Ninety-three percent of pastors reported negative effects from the conflict.

> The collateral damage from conflict falls in two categories. The first is a wounded congregation and pastor, as indicated by damaged relationships, sadness, loss of trust, and bitterness.
>
> The second major negative effect of conflict is that people leave the church. In nearly four out of ten cases (38 percent) pastors told us they left, at least in part, due to conflict. Church leaders leave a third of the time. One-third experienced a drop in church attendance. . . .
>
> Eight in ten pastors experienced conflict aimed at them individually, and right now 13 percent are the focus of direct personal conflict.[32]

One thoughtful observer, who has worked for many years with churches concerned about membership loss, stated that while there are as many stories as there are people, a common thread runs through them all. An event or pattern of events occurred that made them feel unwelcome. Often frenemy fire—either accidental or intentional—played a part.[33]

Universal problem

Frenemy fire is a universal problem. It started in heaven and found its way to earth. You see it at the start of Genesis and can trace it all the way to the close of Revelation. It has found its way into almost every life, family, ministry, and church throughout the history of this world. It has affected you, and it has affected me.

If you've been "shot in the back," you understand the tidal wave of churning thoughts and emotions that threatens to drown you. *This isn't really happening! It must be a bad dream. I feel cornered. What will I do? How will I respond? Am I going to die?*

---

31. *Your Church,* November/December 2005. Christianity Today, Inc.
32. Ibid., January/February 2006.
33. Lewis Wilkins, The Plains Institute LLC, Thursday, August 19, 2004.

CHAPTER 1
SHOT IN THE BACK
Questions to Consider for Personal Inventory or Group Discussions

1. Are you presently engaged in frenemy fire behind someone's back?
2. When talking about someone with whom you disagree, do you use innuendos, half-truths, strange reports, and broken confidences?
3. Would those who know you best say you are domineering and like to control others?
4. Are the emotions of jealousy, envy, and pride well-known in your heart? If so, toward whom are they directed?
5. Would others say you resort to compulsion and force when you don't get your own way?
6. Have you "rubbed out" someone who sees things differently—theologically or philosophically—from the way you do?
7. Who would others say is the one in charge in your life? You or God?
8. Is your spirit one of liberty or control?
9. What is the Spirit of the Lord saying to you in this chapter?
10. Could any of your former associates or those with whom you have had relationships justly use the term *frenemy* in reference to you?

Am I Going to Die?

How long shall I take counsel in my soul, having sorrow in my heart daily?
—Psalm 13:2

Those ten days of waiting seemed like an eternity to me. I rode the full gamut of the emotional roller coaster—from hope to fear, from sorrow to anger, from despair to longing. It felt as if my life was coming to an end. My mind sorted through a dozen different responses as I met my frenemies in my imagination. I knew that it wasn't safe to follow the instincts of my emotions, but what *was* the safe course to follow? How could I sort it all out?

Run and hide!

At one point, I wanted to run and hide. "Lord, whisk me off to a South Pacific island! Let me live in the quiet sunshine away from all the attacks, the turmoil, and the ugliness. Let me hide there until it all settles down and goes away!"

After all, Jesus said, " 'When they persecute you in this city, flee to another.' "[1] Jesus Himself resorted to this response. He transferred His ministry to Galilee because the Jews in Judea were out for His blood.[2] On other occasions, Jesus spoke plain, cutting truths and then departed to hide Himself.[3] Surely I could do the same!

---

1. Matthew 10:23, NKJV.
2. See John 7:1.
3. See John 12:36; Matthew 15:21.

David ran to the wilderness to hide from King Saul. He also fled Jerusalem to avoid a bloody confrontation with his rebel son, Absalom.[4] Elijah was directed by God to hide by the brook Cherith to avoid the malice of Ahab and his cronies.[5] And when the brook dried up, he moved on to hide in Zarephath.[6] Paul, the mighty missionary, often aborted his plans in one region and moved to another because of opposition.[7] That South Pacific island was looking better and better!

Then I thought of Jonah. Jonah ran from opposition, but instead of a South Pacific island, he found himself in the belly of a whale. Elijah ran from Jezebel and found himself hiding in a cave, discouraged and wanting to die. David ran to the Philistines and found himself acting like a madman.[8]

What makes the difference? How do you know when it's right to hide and when it's not?

I decided that it boils down to motive. *Why* do you do what you do? Most of us avoid this kind of heart searching. We're more comfortable with rationalization. We have Scripture to back up why we do what we do—and we stop there. But God isn't fooled.

Jesus in Galilee, David in the wilderness of Judea, Elijah by the brook Cherith, and Paul moving from place to place all had one thing in common: They were pursuing their God-given duty. Jonah in the belly of the whale, Elijah in the cave, and David in Gath also had one thing in common: a strong drive for self-protection.

What about you? Are you pursuing your South Pacific island? Why? Maybe you're like a friend of mine who is facing some friendly fire. She doesn't feel she deserves that South Pacific island. Instead, she craves a deep, dark hole to curl up in with a rock to cover the entrance until the pain is past.

Hiding out of self-protection does not solve problems or develop character. It only allows the problems to snowball. If you find yourself driven by self-protection, you will find God bending over you as

---

4. See 2 Samuel 15:23.
5. See 1 Kings 17:2–6.
6. See 1 Kings 17:9, 10.
7. See Acts 14:6, 20.
8. See 1 Samuel 21:10–15.

He did over Elijah, inquiring, "What are you doing here?"[9]

As I weighed my option of a South Pacific island, I realized that my motive for running would be self-protection—not duty. "OK, Lord. I won't run and hide. But what should I do? I feel like this thing is going to kill me. Maybe I should just capitulate."

Capitulate

Capitulate is a term not heard much today. Its dictionary definition is "to surrender, to give in to an argument, request, pressure, or something unavoidable."[10]

Can this option work to end conflict and bring about peace? Sometimes it does. Paul capitulated to his Jewish brethren and had his friend, Timothy, circumcised to avoid unnecessary quarrelling even though he knew that circumcision was not a moral issue.[11] Jeremiah urged Zedekiah, king of Judah, to capitulate to Nebuchadnezzar to save his people from the horrors of a siege.[12] When the Axis powers in World War II capitulated to the Allies, the bloody war came to an end, and reconstruction of civilized life began.

The Scriptures urge "if it be possible, as much as lieth in you, live peaceably with all men."[13] There is a proper place to concede to the wishes of another, to lay aside our preferences for the mutual benefit of the relationship.[14] We need far more of this kind of capitulation. How much friendly fire would never be launched if we possessed an attitude of kindness and consideration for the opinions and preferences of others? How many church battles over the color of the carpet could be avoided? How many marital falling-outs over burnt toast might be missed? How many alienated friendships might be whole had we not insisted on majoring on the minor and expecting "them" to be like "us"? Yes, it would be a better world if there were more of this kind of capitulation.

---

9. See 1 Kings 19:9.
10. *Encarta® World English Dictionary,* s.v. "Capitulate," http://encarta.msn.com/dictionary_/capitulate.html.
11. See Acts 16:3.
12. See Jeremiah 27:12, 13.
13. Romans 12:18.
14. See Philippians 2:3.

I considered my situation. Maybe I should just give in to my frenemies' demands. Maybe I should just shelve the book and end the conflict. After all, "blessed are the peacemakers."[15] Many would view this as the Christlike response. But would it be? Would it truly bring peace? Was that the real issue?

There is another side to capitulation. Christ could have ended His conflict with the devil in the wilderness by surrendering.[16] And we would all have been lost forever—caught in the hopeless whirlpool of independence from God. Jesus Himself warned, "Think not that I am come to send peace on earth: I came not to send peace, but a sword." "And a man's foes shall be they of his own household."[17]

The Protestants of the Reformation era found themselves locked in deadly conflict. They were usually offered two options—be burned alive at the stake or capitulate. In other words, you are compelled to submit to those who have attacked, besieged, and assaulted you. If you surrender your liberty of conscience and live an overshadowed existence, then there will be so-called peace.

Jerome, the student and friend of John Huss, heard about the impending execution of his master by the Council of Constance. He traveled alone to Constance without a safe-conduct to do what he could to intervene. Arriving there, he discovered that his master's fate was already sealed and that he had placed himself in mortal danger. While attempting to return home, he was noticed and arrested, thrown into a foul dungeon, chained in an unnatural position, and fed on bread and water. After a few months of this treatment, he became very ill, and his enemies, fearing he would escape them through death, eased up a bit—although he remained imprisoned for nearly a year.

Finally he was brought to trial—not the kind of trial you would expect. He was given no opportunity to speak in his defense or to have an advocate or call witnesses. He was simply given a choice—recant or burn. Weakened by illness and the rigors of his prison house, worn down by the torture of anxiety and suspense, separated from his friends, and disheartened by the death of Huss, Jerome's fortitude gave way. He

---

15. Matthew 5:9.
16. See Matthew 4:1–11.
17. Matthew 10:34, 36.

capitulated. He pledged himself to adhere to the Catholic faith and accepted the action of the council in condemning the doctrines of Wycliffe and Huss.[18]

His enemies were delighted—but not satisfied. They tossed him back into his dungeon, and there Jerome saw more clearly what he had done. He thought of the courage and fidelity of Huss, and in contrast pondered his own denial of the truth. He thought of the divine Master whom he had pledged himself to serve, and who for his sake had endured the death of the cross. Before his retraction he had found comfort, amid all his sufferings, in the assurance of God's favor; but now remorse and doubts tortured his soul. He knew that still other retractions must be made before he could be at peace with Rome. His oppressors would never be satisfied until they had complete control of his conscience. The path upon which he was entering could end only in complete apostasy.[19]

Jerome learned by experience that capitulating to those who desire to dominate the conscience brings only a temporary cease-fire. The peace enjoyed is outward only and short-lived. It whets the appetite of the oppressor for further oppression and enables evil to grow. It is not a true solution—only a Band-Aid.

For nearly twelve hundred years the Waldenses advocated the pure gospel of Jesus Christ. They endured torture, persecution, and imprisonment—unspeakable horrors at the hands of those who wanted to control them. Finally, however, they capitulated to the terms of Rome. Peace came to their valleys, but the Spirit left their hearts.

There is a time to surrender—to capitulate—and there is a time to hold steady in the conflict. How do you know which is which? Again—what is the motive? When Jerome capitulated for fear of the flames, he lost his peace with God. There is that self-protection again! Whoever seeks to save his life will lose it. But he who loses it for the sake of Jesus and the gospel shall find it. When Paul capitulated regarding a nonmoral issue for the sake of promoting brotherly unity, he honored God.

---

18. See Emile Bonnechose, *The Reformers Before the Reformation,* vol. 2, p. 141. Cf. Ellen White, *The Great Controversy,* p. 111.

19. See Emile Bonnechose, *The Reformers Before the Reformation,* vol. 2, p. 141. Cf. *The Great Controversy,* p. 111.

If capitulation puts God on the throne of my heart, does not require the sacrifice of moral principle, and opens the way for genuine understanding with another, then it is a good thing. But if capitulation requires the sacrifice of moral principle and places another in charge of my conscience, it is to be shunned.

Jesus said that He came not to bring peace, but a sword and that a man's enemies would be those of his own household.[20] The destructive variety of capitulation is far more common than you might think. How many wives capitulate their individuality to an overbearing husband because they fear the battle that would take place if they were to follow God fully? How many husbands yield their sense of duty because to pursue it would unbalance a self-centered wife? How many children pursue occupations for which they are not suited because they have capitulated to parents who felt it was their place to dominate the conscience of their child?

As I contemplated shelving my writing project, I recognized that I would be doing so out of the desire for peace—for self-protection—and that it would require setting aside a duty God had very clearly laid on my conscience. To capitulate would be to accept man in the place of God. No, capitulation was not my answer. But the urge to protect myself still rose up like a tidal wave. "Oh, Lord, may I defend myself? May I fight back?"

Attack

Charge! Draw the sword. Fight fire with fire. After all, there is "a time to kill . . . and a time to hate."[21] Moses ordered the execution of three thousand Israelites who wouldn't surrender their worship of the golden calf.[22] God told Joshua to wipe out the inhabitants of Canaan.[23] He told Saul to take revenge on the Amalekites for pouncing on the Israelites while they were crossing the desert.[24]

Shouldn't I be a man and stand for my cause? Shouldn't I bring my opponents to their knees? Why not give them a taste of what they were dishing out to me and let them see how it feels?

---

20. See Matthew 10:34, 36.
21. Ecclesiastes 3:3, 8.
22. See Exodus 32:27.
23. See Joshua 1:2–5.
24. See 1 Samuel 15:2, 3.

And so brother rises against brother, church against church, and nation against nation. Self-justification runs strong. Both sides *know* they're right and invoke God's blessing upon themselves. Neither will yield. Bloodshed. Character assassination. We become like cannibals feasting upon the still trembling flesh of our own kind.

David was a warrior. God blessed his battles. God was with him as he fought. God gave him victory over his enemies. But David came close to stepping over a line. While foraging for a living in the wilderness with his band of men, he did a favor for one of the country nobility, Nabal. He protected his flocks from predators and thieves. When shearing time came, David and his men were in desperate need of provisions. David sent one of his men to request assistance from Nabal, pointing out the help they had rendered him earlier. Nabal very curtly and rudely refused David's request, and David got hot. Without consulting God, he prepared for battle. He intended to wipe out every male member of Nabal's household—and he would have done so if Nabal's wife, Abigail, had not heard about the incident.

She set out to meet David with the provisions that he sorely needed and tactfully reasoned with him. She urged him to fight "the battles of the LORD" rather than avenge personal insult.[25]

There's the line: fighting the battles of the Lord versus avenging ourselves. When we fight the battles of the Lord, we are following the One who *laid down* His life and reputation for those who crucified Him— quite a different picture from *defending* my own life and reputation. Again, the issue is God-given duty versus self-protection.

"Lord, my emotions would like to draw the sword. But I've given the reins of my life to You. Are You asking me to fight?"

"No, Jim. I'm asking you to face the situation, trusting Me."

Face it!

Ouch. That touches a tender spot. "No self-protection, Lord? But I think I'll die if I just face it. I'll be so vulnerable, so weak!"

"Let go of your self-protection, Jim. I will be your Shield. Put your trust in Me."

---

25. See 1 Samuel 25:28–31.

"But Lord . . . lay down my hurt? Lay down my anger? Lay down my despair? Those emotions are so strong right now—they feel like they're part of me. To lay them down will feel like death. I can't face it, Lord."

Jim, I'm calling you to change channels. I want you to take your eyes off your circumstances and place them on Me. I'm bigger than it all. I can keep you through it all. The fire need only burn the dross of your character—it need not consume you. Will you face it in My strength and under My direction?"

My will trembled between the gentle, stabilizing call of God's Spirit and the wild churning of my own emotions. Would I trust God? I wanted to—but I felt so weak.

Elijah faced Ahab on Mount Carmel—one lone man against the entire nation. Or so it appeared. But Elijah knew that one man following God on principle was the majority. And God did not fail him.[26]

Jesus faced Calvary—one lone Man under the thumb of pretentious perjury. He knew that one Man doing the will of God from principle would amount to far more than all the pharisaical parades the Jews could conjure up. Through His death, He conquered all and lives today.

Luther faced the Diet of Worms—one lone man against the collusion of empire and ecclesiastical hierarchy. He knew that one man with a conscience void of offense before God and man counted more than a thousand capitulations to maintain the status quo. His quiet affirmation of the right of a person to his own conscience before God sparked a torch of religious liberty that still burns today.

Jerome faced the very council to which he had capitulated. He had made a firm resolution: He would not deny his Lord to escape a brief period of suffering. Surprising all, he firmly and clearly renounced his former recantation—and was erelong condemned to the same fate as Huss.

"He went singing on his way, his countenance lighted up with joy and peace. . . . When the executioner, about to kindle the pile, stepped behind him, the martyr exclaimed: 'Come forward boldly; apply the fire before my face. Had I been afraid, I should not be here.' "[27]

---

26. See 1 Kings 18.

27. Ellen G. White, *The Great Controversy* (Nampa, Idaho: Pacific Press® Publishing Association, 2005), p. 115.

I knew that my meeting was not Mount Carmel or Calvary or the Diet of Worms or the Council of Constance. But it felt like it! Face it? How could I? I couldn't. It was too hard, too devastating. I knew it would be too humiliating to endure, too emotionally draining to handle.

"Lord, I don't have the strength, the words, or the abilities to enter this arena. It's unknown to me. My mind will short-circuit. My tongue will stammer and stutter. I haven't the courage or strength. At times, it seems that death would be a welcome escape. Lord, I'm not a Luther!"

"Jim, you need to face it."

CHAPTER 2

AM I GOING TO DIE?

Questions to Consider for Personal Inventory or Group Discussions

1. Have you allowed your mind to run the emotional roller-coaster ride in response to your experience with frenemy fire?
2. Is your problem-solving technique to run and hide? Or is God directing you to take a furlough?
3. Is the motive for your response self-protection or God-given duty?
4. When others see you, do they want to run and hide?
5. Is God calling you to surrender your positions and capitulate to the demands of others?
6. Could a mutual benefit be derived by conceding your preferences over a nonmoral issue? If so, why not try it?
7. Do you seek vengeance in your thoughts or actions?
8. Are you more like Nabal, David, or Abigail?
9. Are you fighting the battles of the Lord or avenging yourself?
10. Is God asking you to lay down your hurt, your anger, and your despair—and face them?
11. Are you able to trust God in all things?

Facing Your
Firing Squad

When you pass through the waters, I will be with you;
And through the rivers, they shall not overflow you.
When you walk through the fire, you shall not be burned,
Nor shall the flame scorch you.
—Isaiah 43:2, NKJV

I resolved to trust God. I resolved to lay aside my self-protective instincts and cooperate with God to seek His honor. With my emotions still clamoring against the choice of my will, I dialed the church official who I had been told was to be at the meeting.

"Yes, Jim," he confirmed. "One of your ministry associates has invited me to this meeting. He is the one who is initiating it."

"Sir," I asked, "what are your thoughts about a meeting like this—planned by my own ministry associates behind my back for the purpose, I presume, of discrediting me and my book with my publisher—with no opportunity for me to clarify their concerns. Is that right, proper, or fair?"

"Well, Jim, you'll have to take that up with your associate. I'm only an invited guest."

Hanging up the phone, I knelt down. "Lord, this is going to be a difficult conversation. My flesh would like to vent on him and call him to account. But I've decided not to follow my flesh. I will follow You. How would You have me talk with my associate?"

"Jim, approach him mildly and honestly. Tell him what you know and give him the opportunity to explain his actions to you."

Rising from my knees, I called my associate. Calmly, I explained to him that I had learned of the meeting planned with my publisher for December 19. Instantly, I could sense a chill of apprehension over the phone.

"Who has talked to you about this?" he wanted to know.

"My publisher called me, and I called the church official you have invited."

He asked a few more questions and kept his comments very brief.

"Lord, he's not coming clean with me. I'd like to interrogate him and get to the bottom of this thing. I'd like, at least, to put him in his place."

"Jim, surrender those desires to Me. There's no point in accusing or engaging in recriminations. Just stay calm."

My associate obviously wanted to find out as much as possible about what I knew while divulging to me as little as possible. He hadn't wanted me to know about the meeting—and he especially didn't want me to attend the meeting. Finally, I told him that my publisher would not be present at the meeting unless I was present.

He was not pleased. His Plan A was foiled. Evidently, he had wanted to express his point of view to my publisher with no opportunity for another viewpoint to be heard. Our conversation ended coolly.

Plan B

I pursued my day with a strange mixture of turbulent emotions held in check by the peace of God. My mind kept bringing up, "What if . . . " and God kept responding, *"Trust Me, Jim. Rest in Me."*

Finally the phone rang, and I was informed of Plan B. I could attend the meeting on two conditions: I must agree not to speak during the meeting, and I must bring no one with me.

Instantly, my sense of justice rebelled. My work and my life were being called into question. But I wouldn't be able to explain possible misconceptions or clarify facts. Why wouldn't they *want* to understand? Were they trying to arrive at truth or not?

"Lord, why are they playing so unfairly? Who are they to set up such inequitable rules? Lord, this just isn't fair!"

"Jim, it wasn't fair for Me, either."

"Oh Lord, save me from my sense of justice." Calm returned to my heart. "Lord, what would You have me to do?"

"Appeal to their reason and common sense, Jim."

I dialed my publisher.

"Sir, I'm very troubled about the procedure for this meeting. It's evident that those who are planning it didn't want me to know about it, and they don't want any input other than what they plan to present. That hardly seems fair, does it?"

"Well, Jim, we aren't running the meeting. Our only stipulation was that you be at the meeting. Beyond that, you will have to take it up with your associate."

I realized that my publisher was being cautious. He didn't know what kind of information might be forthcoming. Perhaps I was embezzling funds or molesting children or cheating on my wife. I couldn't blame him for his caution, and I appreciated the fact that he had let me know about the meeting and had insisted that I be there—but the unfairness of the whole thing still rankled me.

I ended the conversation with my publisher and called the church official again.

"Are you aware that I can now attend this meeting but that I am not to speak or bring anyone with me?" I asked.

"Yes, I'm aware of that."

"Does that sound fair to you? I mean, isn't that a bit one-sided?"

"Like I told you before, Jim, I'm not the one planning the meeting."

"Are you serious? This sounds to me like nothing more than a trial. Even the world would give a guy a better shot than this!"

"This is not a trial, Jim. It's only a meeting to share some concerns."

In my mind I responded, *That's like telling the victims of the French Revolution that they're only being enrolled in a weight-loss program. It doesn't matter what you label it, the guillotine is still the guillotine.*

Out loud I replied, "You can call it whatever you choose, but the deliberate attempt to keep me from even knowing about the meeting and then refusing to let me speak or bring anyone with me—that doesn't quite have the feel of a friendly sharing of concerns."

"Jim, let me call your associate and see what I can work out. As I said before, I'm not running the meeting; I'm only an invited guest."

I hung up the phone, and another wave of horrendous emotions washed over me. What do I accept? How much do I give in? The apostle Paul came to mind. He had been unjustly beaten and thrown into prison. When God intervened on his behalf, he didn't consent to the magistrate's plea to slip quietly out of town. Rather, he insisted on fair treatment.[1]

"OK, Lord, I'll do all in my power to get as fair a shake as possible."

In the midst of this, I was still working through the aftermath of my younger brother's untimely death and trying to visit with Sally's mother. I was also at the lowest point of physical health that I have ever been in my life. I was sleeping an average of only two or three hours a night. My body was exhausted, and my brain felt like mush.[2] I felt trapped in a tremendous tug-of-war of conflicting emotions. My mind went through my options a thousand times or more. Run and hide? Capitulate? Attack? Face it? Over and over, God brought me back to face it.

"How, Lord? It's just not fair!"

"You're not in this alone, Jim. Rely on Me. My grace is sufficient. You've tested it in the crucible of your home; you've preached it from the pulpit; you've encouraged others to rely on it. I know this is a hard test, but My grace is still sufficient for you."

"But how, Lord? How do I survive this?"

"One moment at a time, Jim. Rely on Me one moment at a time."

Pilgrim's Progress aptly portrays grace one moment at a time. Christian was touring the Interpreter's house and saw a fire burning in front of a wall. A brute of a man dumped bucket after bucket of water on the fire, trying to extinguish it. The fire sizzled and smoked and sputtered, but then always flared up again brightly. To Christian, this was a great mystery. What kept the fire burning? Looking behind the wall, he saw another man pouring oil into a little tube that fed the fire. Interpreter explained that the man behind the wall was Christ who is always near—even when we can't see Him. The oil of His grace is sufficient to sustain us in spite of all the brutal attempts of the enemy to put out the fire.

"OK, Lord. I'll rely on You one moment at a time. I'll trust You to keep feeding in the oil of Your grace one moment at a time."

---

1. See Acts 16:35–39.

2. I have since discovered that I was suffering from a major deficit of key hormones that the body requires to function effectively.

Plan C

The next morning I received another call. I was told there would be seven people at the meeting who would share their concerns about me and my work. Each would be given fifteen minutes to speak. I would be given one fifteen-minute slot to respond. The order of speakers would be determined alphabetically, and since "Hohnberger" was second in alphabetical order, I would be the second person to speak.

At first, this sounded like progress, but I quickly saw problems. How could I share my thoughts effectively without even knowing what I was being accused of and what my accusers were going to say? How would my publisher be able to see the real picture if only one side was presented? Why wouldn't my accusers let me clarify the issues brought up by each speaker? Why wouldn't they let me bring key persons that could give balance to what was presented?

No individual, at least in the United States of America, is put on trial without knowing the accusations against him, without the opportunity of speaking in his own defense, without being able to bring his own witnesses. Meeting? This wasn't a meeting! They could call it a meeting, but it felt like a firing squad!

I didn't believe this was happening! *Will someone please wake me up from this bad dream or at least pinch me or throw some cold water on me? This is a setup. It is all about achieving a predetermined agenda.*

"I appreciate the opportunity to speak," I told my caller, "but I still must object to these unbalanced procedures. How can I adequately answer the accusations brought against me under these conditions? Regardless of what you say, this is looking more and more like an unfair trial."

My heart was aching, and my head was pounding. How could friends, associates, and Christians be so unfair, so unjust, so premeditated? How could those with whom I had worshiped, preached, and socialized be so one-sided, so unreasonable, and so determined to not give me an equal opportunity?

I ended the conversation by imploring, "Would you want to be in my shoes? How would you want to be dealt with if you were me? Will you please just pray about this overnight and ask God what He would have you do?"

Plan D

The next morning, the phone rang again.

"Jim, this is the best we can do. Each of the seven individuals will be given fifteen minutes to speak. As soon as each is finished, you will have five minutes to respond. This is the best arrangement we can offer you."

I was silent for a moment as I summarized the situation in my mind. *Let's see. Seven to one. Each of them gets three times the amount of time to present their thoughts as I have to respond. Each of them knows in advance what he is going to say. I'm left guessing, wondering, and conjecturing. I must listen to their presentations, summarize them in my mind, clarify the issues, and respond in a third of the time that they have. No one is permitted to attend with me. I'm allowed to bring no one to give supporting testimony. They say this is being done because they love me and care for me. But this isn't Christian concern. This is frenemy fire!*

My heart cried, "How could they?"

My head screamed, "It's not fair!"

My emotions clamored, "Run, capitulate, attack!"

My God whispered, *"Face it!"*

I told my caller, "I wouldn't miss the meeting for anything."

Later on, I informed my associate that I would be bringing my wife, my two sons, and their wives.

"Jim, no one else is allowed to come on your behalf."

"I'm sorry, but I'm bringing them."

"Jim, they are not allowed to attend."

My Spanish publisher

Sally and I bid farewell to her mother and flew back to our home in Montana. As we counted down the days until the "meeting," I had to wrestle over and over with my strong emotions. Then a little ray of sunshine brightened the bleakness of my horizon. The phone rang yet again. This time, it was my Spanish publisher, good friend, and former neighbor of nearly seven years.

"Jim, I heard about that meeting, and I'm coming!"

"Really? Praise God! How did you manage that? They're not letting just anyone into that meeting!"

"Well, I thought that if this meeting involves one of your publishers, it should involve both of them. As your Spanish publisher, I need to know what their concerns are as well. The only drawback is that they are essentially gagging me. I may sit in on the meeting, but I cannot speak a word on your behalf. That I regret."

"But you're the only one who knows almost all of these people and the behind-the-scenes working of the ministry."

"Precisely, Jim. That's probably why I'm not being allowed to speak."

"Well, why come then?"

"Jim, I want to be there to see it with my own eyes and hear it with my own ears."

What a friend! At his own expense he flew all the way out from the Midwest with no opportunity to ask a question, clarify the facts, or give his testimony. It has often been said that your darkest hour reveals who your true friends really are.

"Oh, Lord, give me a dozen of this kind of friend."

December 19, 2002, 8:30 A.M.

Sally and I, Matthew and Angela, and Andrew and Sarah arrived a few minutes early at the church where the meeting would take place. As we entered the lobby, it felt like the temperature dropped about fifty degrees even though it was winter and the furnace was on. The feelings of apprehension, awkwardness, and tension only heightened when some of our ministry associates approached us, hugged us, and told us that they loved us. Why was that so disgusting to me? Why did my stomach want to erupt?

We were ushered into a small side chapel with pews on both sides. Two of the seven who would speak had brought their wives, and all but one of them sat down on the left side. Sally and I, with our two sons and their wives, our Spanish publisher, and the one remaining speaker sat on the right side. The publisher who had first called me sat in the back on the very last pew and didn't say a word until the meeting was over.

I took a moment to glance around, noting who was present. I hardly knew the one gentleman sitting on the right side of the chapel. I couldn't remember even talking with him for any length of time. Two of the other six were individuals I had rarely seen and had hardly spoken with over the last decade or more. I thought to myself, *This is going to be interesting.*

I sensed an awkwardness with my ministry associate because I had dared to bring my family with me. A discussion ensued, concluding with a secret vote, as to whether my wife, my sons, and their wives would be permitted to remain.

I couldn't believe it! What did they have to hide? Were they that afraid of fairness, equality, and due process? Why did my sense of justice want to protest? Why did my heart want to cry? Why did my mind sense this was a setup?

I remembered Martin Luther. I wondered what it had been like to face his firing squad. Mine seemed much less daunting by comparison. Daniel was hated so much that his firing squad contrived a way to dump him in a lions' den. Wycliffe and Huss had met with far more damaging firing squads than mine. Sure it was unfair. Sure I was outnumbered and outgunned. But there was no changing any of that right now. They said they were my friends, but my son had called them "frenemies." I thought he was right.

But God said, *"Face it."* He also said, *"I will never leave thee, nor forsake thee."*[3] Once again, I surrendered my emotions and thoughts to be governed, not by the situation, but by God. "Lord, I relinquish my reputation to You. I relinquish my very life to You. In fact, death would be a positive alternative here. It doesn't matter what happens to me, Lord. I relinquish myself into Your hands."

The gentleman sitting in front of me, whom I hardly knew, was trying to decide how to vote on the question of whether my family could remain. He turned around to face me with a questioning look on his face. "Jim, why did you bring your family?"

"For moral support," I replied. "Put yourself in my shoes. Wouldn't you want some moral support?"

What I didn't tell him was that I didn't want any questions in my family's minds about their father. I know how innuendos, half-truths, and misinformation work. Lucifer used these weapons in heaven to turn a third of the holy angels against their heavenly Father. I wanted my loved ones to have full disclosure—to witness the events of this day firsthand so there would be no question to linger in their minds.

The vote came in. My wife and sons could stay provided they said nothing. My daughters-in-law would have to leave. They would not be permitted to observe this "Christian meeting." They agreed, although I could see the unfairness registered in their eyes.

---

3. Hebrews 13:5.

As far as I was concerned, the facts were already in. Anyone who could give a balancing statement or a clarifying testimony had either been held to silence or removed from the meeting.

Jesus' trial

I reflected how Jesus' trial was held secretly late at night, with only select individuals attending. He had no one by His side—no one, that is, but His Father. There was no fault in Him. Now me—that's a different story!

I was born disconnected from my Lord. I grew up with my lower nature in charge. For almost four decades it ruled until I began to discover a walk with God that enabled me to live by His Word and empowered me to operate by His Spirit. I know I've fumbled the ball along the way. I know all my dross is not yet burned up. In fact, I was feeling the heat right then. God reminded me again that His grace was sufficient—that the fire would consume only the dross as long as I kept my hand in His. This "meeting," placed in His sovereign hands, could work for my best good.

"OK, Lord. Let's face it together."

The meeting begins

Someone handed me a printed copy of the agenda. As I looked over it, I saw the stated objective of the meeting: "This meeting is for the purpose of expressing concerns and observations about author and speaker Jim Hohnberger in conjunction with the proposed book, *It's About People.*"

The meeting was scheduled to start at 8:30 A.M. and end at 11:00 A.M. I had anticipated what I would be feeling at this moment, but to my surprise no anxiety hung over me. I seemed to have a calmness and rest I had not thought possible. I had even slept fairly well the night before. "Thank You, Lord. You really are in it with me," I breathed.

The meeting was presided over by the church official. Evidently, at the last minute, my ministry associate had asked him to chair the meeting.

Prayer was the first item on the agenda. Each of the seven individuals then presented their concerns. Their presentations varied in length and in depth and brought up issues that would take at least an hour to answer completely. Nevertheless, after each speaker had finished, I stood and tried to clarify my perspective in five minutes or less. My whole goal was simply to give the rest of the story. My wife told me later that she was pleased with the calmness, clarity, and brevity of my responses. At the time I was too much in the thick of things to be able to analyze how effectively I was responding. But God does attend us in our time of trial. In retrospect, I recognized the miracle of His grace subduing the powerful emotions I had wrestled with during the days leading up to this moment.

The meeting turned out to be more difficult for my older son and my Spanish publisher than it was for me. Matthew was so disturbed over some of the misinformation and one-sided presentations he could hardly sit still. He had experienced his own frenemy fire with some of these same individuals. Matthew is a very expressive person with a keen sense of justice. It was almost more than he could handle to sit there and listen without any opportunity to set things straight.

Unbeknown to me, a mutual friend of mine and my ministry partner stood just outside the door and eavesdropped on the whole meeting. Afterward she explained that she just had to hear it for herself. Certainly, she thought, there must be some deep, dark sin in Jim's life to provoke such a meeting. She expected to hear some awful charge brought forward, but no such charge was forthcoming. By the end of the meeting, she was irate. In her view, the accusations were nothing more than an assortment of differing views about how to conduct one's life.

One such issue concerned young people and marriage. Sally and I believe that when children become adults, they become ultimately responsible for their own decisions and actions, that they are free moral agents and can choose the life partners they want to marry.

We believe parents should take the role of a coach—rather than a governor. We encourage young people to counsel with the parents on both sides of the relationship. However, in the end, the final decision rests with the young people themselves; they have the right to decide who and when they will marry, even when one or more of the parents disagrees. Not everyone in this meeting agreed with this view—which had caused a small war between us.

Another issue concerned my reading material. One of my few hobbies is reading literature from the Protestant Reformation of the sixteenth through the eighteenth centuries. Many of the writers of that era wrote from the perspective of discovering the beautiful light of a genuine heart religion against the backdrop of deep doctrinal darkness.

41

Their writings reflect that mixture of truth and error, and my critics were concerned that I might imbibe in and possibly perpetuate those errors.

I believe that reading the works of Luther and Wesley doesn't make me a Lutheran or Methodist any more than reading *National Geographic* makes me an evolutionist. I asked my critics to cite one sentence from any of my books or one statement from the scores of my recorded sermons that would give any evidence supporting their concern. There was none. In the days of the Reformation, people were burned at the stake merely for possessing unauthorized books. Heaven help us if we ever embrace such a misuse of control!

Another called my integrity into question because at times I had misunderstood a question and hadn't always responded just as he would in a given situation. Now I freely admit that I blunder from time to time. God isn't finished with me yet—nor is He finished with any of us. We all must be patient with one another. But I don't believe that the mistakes and blunders common to humanity are necessarily "integrity issues." The dictionary definition of *integrity* is "the quality of possessing and steadfastly adhering to high moral principles or professional standards."[4] David said that he "walked in [his] integrity."[5] In other words, he did not knowingly or willingly violate moral principle. I can honestly state that in the examples cited by my detractors, I had not knowingly or willingly violated any moral principle. I had simply misunderstood the question put to me or responded according to my personality and perspective of the situation.

A couple of other areas concerning the conduct of life were brought forward in which my critics and I had differing views or perspectives—none of which, I believe, involved moral issues or violations of principle.

As the meeting progressed, it became clear to me that the real purpose was not to challenge the message of the book at issue, but rather to discredit the messenger. I now know why the Reformers were almost universally denied time to present their opinions or clarify their stands.

---

4. *Encarta® World English Dictionary*, s.v. "Integrity," http://encarta.msn.com/dictionary_/integrity.html.

5. Psalm 26:1.

Had they been allowed to do so, they would have neutralized the false accusations and exposed the misinformation.

The last of the seven speakers stood and eloquently stated his concerns about me—restating some of the issues mentioned above. He concluded by proposing that not only should *It's About People* not be published but also that the other books I had authored should be pulled from bookstores.

I looked around at the other six. Would any raise an objection to this final proposal? They all sat silently. I could only conclude that they agreed. I stood one last time and briefly explained my thoughts and actions once again. When I sat down, I felt peace wash over my soul. My reputation and my future ministry were in God's hands. If He had further work for me, He could open the way and direct.

Now it was time for my publisher to share his thoughts. Everyone turned around to stare at him. What would be his conclusion? Would he agree with my critics? Would he stop publication of *It's About People*? Would he have my other books withdrawn from circulation? A drumroll would have fit the moment perfectly—at least in my heart!

My publisher rose to his feet and began to speak.

"I'm glad I attended this meeting. It was helpful to be here.

"As a publisher, we have two basic criteria for our authors and their publications. We have various processes we go through to ensure that these criteria are met. The bigger picture for us is that we reflect properly the doctrines and standards of God's church. So, the first question we ask is, 'Is the proposed publication doctrinally sound?'

"The second question is, 'Does the author preach and teach in accordance with sound doctrine? Does he live the life of a Christian? Will he bring disrepute upon the church of Christ?'

"To address the first question, we sent Jim's manuscript to one of the most conservative theologians in the denomination—prior to this meeting and without Jim's knowledge. His response was brief: '*It's About People*—it's about time!' He saw no doctrinal error in the book and gave it a clean bill of health.

"In addressing the second question, we see no evidence that Jim is not living what he is preaching and teaching. As far as we can tell, his lifestyle is in accordance with the standards of the church. The meeting today has simply raised matters of differing personal perspectives on nonessential issues of how to live one's life. These are not our concern."[6]

As the meeting adjourned, the one man I hardly knew drew me aside. "Jim," he began huskily, "I owe you an apology. I was convinced by what the others said that coming here today would be an honorable thing to do. But I was wrong. Will you forgive me?"

"Of course I forgive you," I replied. "Let's each learn from this experience and not repeat it."

I saw this gentleman recently at a social occasion, and he apologized again. "I'm facing my own frenemy fire now, Jim, and I can really empathize with how it must have felt for you. Please forgive me for my part in it."

Today, my path doesn't cross often with those of the other six individuals. I have offered three of them and their families the option of meeting with a neutral biblical reconciliation specialist, but so far they have declined. The door in my heart to this process remains open to all of them.

Personal differences

Why do we dread that which in the end is profitable? That experience did not kill me—as I felt it was going to do. Instead, I learned a great deal.

Most important, I grew in my experience of learning to rest in my Lord. He did not fail me! He was there with me! His grace was sufficient! He provided just what I needed when I needed it! My confidence in Him grew by leaps and bounds.

I gained a graphic glimpse of some of my own dross that needs to be refined. Until you are placed in a position like that, it is hard to imagine how deeply rooted the instinct for self-protection actually is. As I wrestled through the workings of my own mind prior to the meeting, I had to face that instinct and yield my responses to the will of God again and again and again.

My understanding of human relationships also deepened. I recognized that I had confided in some of these seven individuals, assuming that they were friends. I discovered most painfully that some of these

---

6. This publisher did publish *It's About People,* and it became one of the bestsellers for that year.

people misused my confidences in them for their own advantage. I now guard my speech much more judiciously. Today, I don't share certain things until I'm sure of the person's loyalty and integrity.

And last, but not least, I matured in my understanding of how personal conflict is *not* to be handled. There is a biblical way of working through our concerns with each other, and it doesn't require a firing squad.

A firing squad proves nothing and provides no spiritual benefit. I could pick a firing squad of a half-dozen individuals who have concerns—differing perspectives or points of view—about any one of those seven individuals. I could pull a meeting together to discredit them and try to pressure them into conforming to my way of seeing things. We'll never arrive at unity that way—never!

We've got to start coming to a better understanding of the difference between unity and uniformity. In fact, I explore that in detail in the chapter "Unity or Uniformity" in the book *It's About People*.

We do need input from each other. None of us have achieved perfection. We all have character imbalances to which we may be blind, but are clearly apparent to someone else. And there are areas where we sincerely and honestly differ. God has ways for us to work with each other so that our differences enrich us rather than fracture us. "As iron sharpens iron, so a man sharpens the countenance of his friend."[7]

But our manner and approach with each other is crucial. It makes all the difference in the outcome. It also has a major effect upon our witness in this world. Non-Christians are not going to be converted as much by our truth as by how we live the truth with those with whom we disagree. That's what the book *It's About People* is all about. How ironic that the very book that caused this controversy deals with exactly what was happening in that meeting. In fact, right in the heart of the book is quoted a most precious statement:

"There can be no more conclusive evidence that we possess the spirit of Satan than the disposition to hurt and destroy those who do not appreciate our work, or who act contrary to our ideas."[8]

How important for us to evaluate the spirit that is motivating our actions! Trying to set someone straight can look so correct, so right, so pious—and

---

7. Proverbs 27:17, NKJV.
8. Ellen G. White, *The Desire of Ages*, p. 487.

yet the spirit of Satan can actuate it. How can we approach these differences in God's Spirit? We'll explore that question throughout this book.

Your firing squad

I didn't write this book for my benefit. I wrote it for you. When God called me to begin speaking and writing, He impressed upon me that my style should be based on my own experience of applying His principles of living to my life. I have found that in so doing, the reader and the listener are able to enter into it.

Your firing squad will probably differ from mine. It may arise from behind closed doors within your own home. Brother against brother or sister against sister. Mother against father or parent against child. In the church, it finds its way into the nominating committee. People striving for position, control, and influence. At work, it's often over favoritism with the boss, competition for a promotion, or who gets what territory. In friendships, it quite often involves jealousy for first place in someone's relationship or their time. In ministry, it can be for who is seen as the leader, who gets the most speaking slots, or who rates the best billing and public acclaim.

I dare say there are a million and one different scenarios. Nevertheless, they all have certain characteristics in common. They all begin with some kind of discontented feeling. As that feeling is nurtured, the desire to control—to be in charge—grows. And sooner or later, a firing squad is born.

Your choice

So let's ask ourselves some pertinent questions. Are we participating in any firing squads? Are we nurturing discontented feelings about something or someone? Are we excusing the disposition to take things into our own hands? Who is in charge?

If you are on the other end of the gun, facing that firing squad, how are you responding? Are you running and hiding? Are you capitulating? Are you attacking? Are you facing it?

If you are facing it with your hand in Christ's, you will find that the fire will only burn the dross from your character. It will refine your gold. That's how God uses the ministry of evil.

Joseph faced a very damaging firing squad. His own brothers sold

---

9. Genesis 50:20, NKJV.

him out. But he faced it with God in charge of his life. When it was all said and done, he could look his frenemies in the eyes and say, " 'You meant evil against me; but God meant it for good.' "[9]

Nothing can touch our lives unless it first passes through the throne of grace. That was true in the unfairness of Joseph's life, Jesus' life, the Waldenses, Huss, Jerome, Wycliffe, Luther, and perhaps you and me. Not that we rank with these "big ones." But surely in our own little worlds, God is calling each of us to stand for His principles by His power and for His honor.

But why does it seem that the other side doesn't *want* to listen? Why are there so many procedural maneuverings? Why are they so afraid of an in-depth investigation? Why is full disclosure of all the facts not allowed? Why is there such an obvious disparity between profession and actions behind the scenes?

CHAPTER 3

FACING YOUR FIRING SQUAD

Questions to Consider for Personal Inventory or Group Discussions

1. Do you know how to lay aside your self-protective instincts and cooperate with God in seeking His honor?
2. Are you able to rise above unfairness? Or does your keen sense of justice get in the way?
3. Is God asking you to pursue fair treatment?
4. By your actions, are you a friend or a frenemy?
5. When you are outgunned and outnumbered, do you sense God's presence by your side?
6. Are you involved in politics against anyone?
7. Do you know how to relinquish yourself, your situation, and your emotions into God's hands?
8. Do you believe that when man shuts a door, God can open a window?
9. Why do you dread that which in the end is profitable to you?
10. Are you willing to grow in the experience of learning to rest completely in your Lord?
11. Are you forming firing squads against others?

A Predetermined Heart

Let us draw near with a true heart . . .
having our hearts sprinkled from an evil conscience.
—Hebrews 10:22

Feeling puzzled, stunned, and forlorn, I returned home. Sure, I was grateful that my publisher hadn't killed *It's About People,* but my mind kept trying to put the pieces of the picture together. Why had this happened?

A jumble of memories from the past couple of years swirled around in my mind, making no sense. They just didn't add up, and I didn't know what to do about it. I was stumped. I needed a time-out—just like in football. When the opposing team has you baffled and on the defensive, you take a time-out to find a new approach. I needed time to consult with my Coach. I knew He had the experience, the wisdom, and the insight I needed. He knows how to direct me for the next play.

During the next week, I took that time-out. I found myself often on my knees or taking long walks. "Lord, I'm confused. I can't seem to fix this situation or make any sense of it. Help!"

I began rereading the Gospels with the eyes of a desperate searcher, and what I discovered there not only amazed me, but also opened my understanding.

Two thieves

Hung between heaven and earth, Jesus was flanked by two thieves—both convicted of the same crime, both sentenced to the same hideous death. A bystander would not have distinguished one from the other. But Jesus perceived that one possessed a listening heart and the other a predetermined heart.

I suspect that both thieves had seen Jesus in the judgment hall and on the way to Calvary, and they probably had heard and seen Him as He ministered to the multitudes during His three and a half years of public ministry.

At first, both thieves railed at Him. Suffering caused the one to become more desperate and defiant—a hallmark of the predetermined heart. His mouth was a firing squad, hurling jabs and insinuations at Jesus. He was also quite willing to use Christ for his own advantage. "If thou be the Christ, save thyself and us."[1] Even his own companion could not reason with him.[2] His mind was settled, fixed, predetermined.

This man had much in common with Caiaphas and his kind. They also would have willingly used Jesus for their own advantage. If Jesus had catered to their policy, power, and position, they would have hailed Him as one of their own. They would gladly have followed Him in removing the Romans and conquering the world. But because Jesus pursued hearts rather than ego, influence, or empires, they had no use for Him. They stood around the cross, taking pleasure in His suffering, taunting Him, goading Him, and humiliating Him.

The thief at Jesus' other side watched what was going on. He listened to the gibes of the great religionists and compared them with the testimonies of the passersby who defended Jesus. He saw Jesus submit His strong, muscular body to the mangling of the hammer and nails. He heard Jesus breathe a prayer of forgiveness for His tormentors—even while he himself was cursing in agony. The Holy Spirit formed in his mind a chain of evidence, and he saw in Jesus—bruised, mocked, and hanging upon the cross—the Lamb of God who takes away the sin of the world, *his* sin. Hope mingled with anguish as he cried those unforgettable words full of faith and confidence: "Lord, remember me when thou comest into thy kingdom."[3]

---

1. Luke 23:39.
2. See verses 40, 41.
3. Luke 23:42.

Those two thieves represent you and me. They represent all who have lived upon this earth. All of us have sinned and deserve death. Christ died for all but not all benefit. Why? Because of a predetermined heart.

What about you? What about me?

Which thief represents your experience? I'm sure we all want to identify ourselves with the one who was promised a place in Paradise, but let's look a little deeper.

Do you see some things so confidently, so assuredly, that you leave no room for anyone else to view them differently, understand or teach them differently? Are you so certain of your understanding of the Second Coming, for example, or of lifestyle issues or of standards of child rearing that you start your own little jihad against those who dare to have a different view of these things? Are you so entrenched that no reasoning or evidence can move you? Are you convinced everyone else is wrong? Is it your way or the highway? Are you biased, stubborn, and bullheaded? Do you become hostile, critical, and condemning to the point of cannibalizing someone's reputation? Are you like the institutionalists who stoned Stephen[4]—stiff-necked, unwilling to turn your head toward a deeper understanding of what is true? Are you "uncircumcised in heart and ears," thinking that you know everything and unwilling to listen to any perspective other than your own? If so, you have "stopped your ears" and are resisting the Holy Spirit.[5]

Or are you like Stephen, who faced those angry, predetermined hearts, praying, " 'Lord, do not charge them with this sin' "?[6]

Let's examine the contrasting characteristics below. None of us scores 100 percent on the right side of the chart all of the time, but which side predominates in your life? Go ahead. Ask your spouse, your children, your siblings, your friends, relatives, church members, neighbors, and fellow employees—the ones who'll tell you the truth. Ask them whether you have a predetermined heart or a listening heart. Take a census. Compare it with God's Word and ask His Holy Spirit to speak to your

4. See Acts 7:51–60.
5. See verses 51, 57, NKJV.
6. Verse 60, NKJV.

conscience. If you are predominantly predetermined, most likely your marriage will be stale, your children wounded, and your friends distant or offended. Sure, we all make some bloopers, but which side is prevalent in your life?

Predetermined Heart	Listening Heart
Think "I have it all together."	Admit my weaknesses.
"I don't have all the answers, but let me tell you a thing or two!"	"I am seeking for balance."
Externally religious; play by the rules.	Genuinely spiritual through daily surrender of the heart to God and His Word.
Defensive and self-protective.	Open to feedback.
Self-righteous; can do no wrong.	Humble and meek.
Rarely apologize; don't change.	Truly repentant and make lasting change.
Demand trust and love.	Willing to earn trust and love.
Live for myself.	Sacrifice for others.
Criticize and blame others for my problems.	Shoulder my responsibility.
Intolerant.	Tolerant.
Use deception as a way to manage life and relationships.	Tell the truth and respect the free moral agency of others.
Stagnant.	Growing.
"I'm in charge!"	"God's in charge!"
Avoid intimacy—"into-me-you-see."	Willing to connect and go deep, heart-to-heart.
Concerned only about me.	Concerned about others.
Resist granting liberty to another.	Protect individuality and freedom of conscience.
Condemning; finger-pointing.	Forgiving.
Gossip behind others' backs.	Hold confidences of others.
Political; policy oriented.	Practical; commonsense oriented.
Use position to my own advantage.	Interested in serving rather than ruling.
Self-confident.	Self-distrustful.
My way or the highway.	Show me the way.
Will use you for my own advantage.	Value you for you.
Man-managed.	God-governed.

Is there blood on your sword? If so, you are in need of the blood that was shed that sad day on Golgotha. Let's get down on our knees and surrender all our known choices to Jesus. Let's put up our swords, put away our self-righteousness, and learn to listen with spiritual ears and to love with the divine heart. This is the new heart and right spirit that God is trying to create in us.[7] It is the cure for a predetermined heart. By this shall all men know that we are His disciples—if we love one another.[8] Selfless love, displayed toward one another, witnesses to the world that we are true disciples. If there is no sacrifice, there is no love. Calvary demonstrated the ultimate sacrifice for others.

Who are these others? Those we disagree with. Those who cross us. Those who are impossible to deal with. That spouse who irritates us every day. Those children who get under our skin. Those relatives with whom no one can get along. The gospel is about dying in order to live. Let's take our place with the penitent thief, praying, "Lord, draw me into the fold of Your listening heart that I may love those who persecute me and assassinate my name. Give me not only a mind to know truth, but *ears* to hear Your Spirit instruct me in the way, all day, and a will to follow You. Truth without Your Spirit can be brutal, while relying on Your Spirit without truth can result in mere sensationalism. Give me the balance I'm missing that I may love the unlovable and befriend the friendless."

Which thief am I?

Nothing so clearly reveals the presence of a predetermined heart as contact with a listening heart. Abel's listening heart enraged the predetermined heart of Cain. David's listening heart goaded the predetermined heart of King Saul. The wise men's listening hearts inflamed the predetermined heart of Herod.

Jesus, the ultimate Model of the listening heart, attracted other listening hearts. But those with predetermined hearts were hardened and repelled by Him. What about you? What about me? When the litmus test is applied to us, do we line up with Christ or with Caesar? With principle or with policy? With liberty of conscience or with undue control?

7. See Psalm 51:10.
8. See John 13:35.

We can trace this polarization between listening hearts and predetermined hearts all through Jesus' life right down to the cross:

Predetermined Heart	Listening Heart
Herod the Great (Matthew 2:1–18)	Mary, Jesus' mother (Luke 1; 2)
The scribes and Pharisees (Matthew 23)	The shepherds (Luke 2:8–17)
Jesus' Nazarene neighbors (Luke 4:16–30)	Simeon and Anna (Luke 2:25–38)
The Sanhedrin (John 5)	The paralytic of thirty-eight years (John 5)
The nine lepers (Luke 17:11–19)	The one leper (Luke 17:11–19)
The chief priests and elders (John 11:46–54)	Mary Magdalene, Martha, and Lazarus (John 11:1–44)
The Samaritans (Luke 9:51–53)	The Syro-Phoenician woman (Mark 7:24–30)
The rich young ruler (Matthew 19:16–22)	The demon-possessed man (Mark 1:23–27)
The multitudes who followed Jesus for the loaves and fishes (John 6:26, 66)	The little children who came for Jesus' blessing (Mark 10:13–16)
Judas (Mark 14:10, 11)	Blind Bartimaeus (Mark 10:46–52)
Annas and Caiaphas (John 18:13–24)	Nicodemus (John 3:1–21; 7:50–53; 19:39)
Pontius Pilate (John 18:28–19:19)	Levi-Matthew (Luke 5:27–32)
Herod the Tetrarch (Luke 23:8–12)	The woman at the well (John 4:5–30)
The thief on the cross (Luke 23:39)	The other thief on the cross (Luke 23:40–43)

One focus

As I pondered the contrast between the predetermined heart and the listening heart, my mind began to wrestle with how Jesus dealt with each. It began to dawn on me why Jesus' approach varied so often with different people. He was wise, yet discriminating; noncondemning, while revealing the secrets of the heart; approachable, yet challenging. While stirring up deep controversy, He never entered into controversy. While making strong appeals to the conscience, He never forced obedience. While presenting compelling arguments, He never compelled agreement. I saw that in all His interactions with others Jesus had one focus: to awaken the listening heart. And when it was awakened, He deepened conviction, encouraged faith, and strengthened resolve. If it could not be awakened, He often didn't answer His questioners, bypassing their interrogations or changing the subject.

One day a group of Pharisees and scribes approached Him, dragging with them a terror-stricken woman whom they openly accused of having committed adultery.[9] They had "truth" on their side; they had the establishment on their side; they had the "law" on their side. They drew themselves up in their robes of piety and challenged, "Moses in the law commanded us, that such should be stoned: but what sayest thou?"[10]

Jesus saw that this was a setup designed to gather ammunition for a firing squad to accuse Him. Their hearts were conniving, fixed, stubborn, and predetermined. Jesus' interest, however, was neither to counterattack nor to run from the firing squad but to draw out the listening heart.

He knew the accused woman had such a heart. She stood there cowering with fear, cringing in anticipation of the first stone. Consumed with feelings of guilt, shame, and embarrassment, she hardly noticed that her accusers were disappearing, one by one. Finally, Jesus quietly asked, "Woman, where are those thine accusers? hath no man condemned thee?" Timidly raising her eyes and glancing around her, she replied, "No man, Lord." And Jesus tenderly bade her, "Neither do I condemn thee: go, and sin no more."[11] In this woman, He found the listening heart.

Not so with the Pharisees. Seeming not to have heard them at their first approach, Jesus had stooped and begun writing on the ground with His finger. That irked them to no end. They demanded His attention. "So when they continued asking him, he lifted up himself, and said unto them, He that is without sin among you, let him first cast a stone at her."[12]

And bending over again, He continued writing. The Scriptures don't tell us what He wrote, but I believe He was writing their personal sins on the ground. Whatever it was, it was enough to silence these demand-

9. See John 8:1–11.
10. Verse 5.
11. Verses 10, 11.
12. Verse 7.

ing religionists. As they read the inscriptions, they were convicted by their own conscience and left one by one, beginning with the oldest down to the youngest. What they saw convinced them that Jesus was capable of exposing far more to the crowd than they ever cared to admit. Unwilling to confess their treachery and yield to conviction, they hurriedly fled the scene. Jesus had called for a listening heart, but their predetermined stance locked Him out.

The predetermined heart loves to engage in endless arguments, discussions, entrapments, and debates that only go in circles. You can't reason through the problem; you can't arrive at a solution; you can't fix it. You can pour your heart, your energy, your very soul into the problem and still find yourself back where you started—or worse, totally derailed from the path of common sense, principled reasoning, and Spirit-led solutions.

Jesus faced the predetermined heart again and again. He always refused to get into a discussion with such individuals. He rarely answered their questions directly. More often, He would ask them a question in return to provoke deeper thought.[13] He told them stories—leading them to pronounce judgment on themselves.[14] At times He was silent—even seemingly cool and impolite.[15] At other times He confronted them with scathing rebukes.[16]

Toward the end of His ministry, He even preached an entire sermon about the predetermined heart—not out of bitterness but because the predetermined heart can be so confusing to deal with.[17] He advised his listeners to observe what those with predetermined hearts asked of them as long as it was in accord with principle, but not to follow their example. While zealous to promote their religion, they only worsen the lives of their converts. While pretending to be very pious in externals, they avoid duties that require the denial of self. While straining at a gnat, they swallow a camel. They are like a whitewashed tomb—clean and attractive on the outside, but full of death on the inside—and unwilling to exchange their condition for a new life.

---

13. See Matthew 15:1–9; Luke 20:1–8.
14. See Matthew 21:33–46.
15. See Luke 23:9; Mark 14:60, 61.
16. See Matthew 23:27, 28.
17. See Matthew 23.

Speak to me, Lord!

Jesus' wisdom to His twelve trainees was, "Let them alone: they be blind leaders of the blind."[18] "Give not that which is holy to the dogs, neither cast ye your pearls before swine, lest they trample them under their feet, and turn again and rend you."[19] Why? Because it accomplishes nothing good to play their game. They will not value the pearls of your time, perspective, energy, or individuality. They will only use them to mire you deeper in the muck. The more you touch it and enter into it, the stickier it gets.

I'm learning from experience and from Jesus' example to inquire, "Lord, do they have a predetermined heart like Pharaoh[20] or a listening heart like the three wise men?[21] Speak to me, Lord. Show me by their words, their actions, their countenance, and their fruit whether they have a predetermined heart or a listening heart. Then show me what You would have me to do.[22] Lord, I'm like a babe in the woods. Lead me like a blind man through this maze. Give me Your wisdom, Your eyes, and Your heart to live as You lived."

A dream from God?

Sam, an acquaintance, called me on the phone the other day. "Jim," he said, "I've had an amazing dream I'd like to share with you. I'd like to know what you think of it."

"OK, Sam. Go ahead."

"Well, Jim, I have been praying for a long time that God would give me something bigger to do for Him than I've ever done before. The other night I had a dream that leads me to believe that He is calling me to leave everything behind and throw myself into speaking and ministering to other people's health." He shared the details of his dream and then asked, "Jim, do you think this is God calling me?"

"Sam, that dream could come from either God or Satan, and I don't know which. With your permission, I'd like to ask you some questions before I say anything."

18. Matthew 15:14.
19. Matthew 7:6.
20. See Exodus 7–14.
21. See Matthew 2:1–12.
22. See Acts 9:6.

"Sure, Jim. Go ahead."

"Are you presently employed?"

There was a bit of a pause. Then he answered, "No."

"How long have you been out of work?"

Another pause. "A year and a half."

"How are you supporting your family?" I sensed he was getting uncomfortable. He certainly wasn't as expressive as he had been in telling me about his dream.

"Oh, we're getting by!"

"Lord," I prayed silently, "should I go on?"

Keep probing gently, Jim.

"Sam, how is your relationship with your wife? What does she think of this dream?"

"Why are you questioning me in these areas?" Sam was beginning to sound a little self-protective.

"I'm just wondering if you are living up to the light you presently have."

A long moment went by before Sam mumbled, "Well, no. Not really."

"One more question. When you share this dream with those who know you the best, what is their response?"

Sam's voice got rather belligerent. He became defensive, justifying himself, and making excuses. I noted mentally how quickly his attitude toward me had changed.

To test the waters, I briefly changed my direction and style. "In spite of what you've told me," I said, "this dream could possibly still be from God."

Instantly he warmed up. The barriers came down, and he started sharing that he felt God was calling him. Now I knew I was talking to a man with a predetermined heart. When I expressed agreement with him, he was friendly, warm, and enthusiastic. However, as soon as I shared insights from past experience that might illustrate principles to guide his evaluation of the dream, he got cold, abrasive, and almost ready to attack.

I proceeded to share with him the principle that God usually has us first put our base camp in order and that this qualifies us experientially to work on the front lines. I cited the thirty quiet years Jesus spent at home preparing for His three and a half years of public ministry. I discussed Moses herding sheep for forty years until he saw his ineffectiveness, unworthiness, and lack of self-confidence. Only then did God call him into full-time ministry. I mentioned Saul's three years in the wilderness of Arabia before he became Paul the great evangelist. This all seemed to fall on deaf ears. However, when I talked about how Jesus gave Peter, James, and John on-the-job training, his hearing picked up.

What did that tell me? It told me that Sam wanted only my rubber stamp of approval—not my honest opinion. Did I really know whether God was calling him into this ministry? No. But that wasn't the point. The point was (and is) that God tries to save us from a lot of dead ends, heartache, discouragement, argument, and wasted time, energy, and emotion. He wants us to test the waters, try the spirits. If there is no real, practical, or logical openness, then we should let these individuals alone—at least for the time being. Why? Because they don't have a listening heart!

This is a hard thing to do—hard because there are a lot of situations that you simply cannot change or bring balance to. If you are like me, a "fix-it" kind of person, it's very frustrating to just leave situations or individuals in God's hands. But that's Jesus' example. He knew that debate, compulsion, controversy, and behind-the-scenes maneuvering only exacerbate the situation. Often, you will have opportunity to interact with that person again and test the waters to see if there is any softening in the predetermined heart. If not, there is no point in ramming your head against a brick wall. Your God will direct you. His Holy Spirit will impress you. His Word will convict you as to which kind of heart you are dealing with and what He would have you to do in each situation.

Predetermined at home

One of the most difficult places to face a predetermined heart is in your own home—with your own spouse. That's the predicament in which Jerry found himself. He had met Linda at a time in his life when he was particularly vulnerable. Linda was warm, generous, and caring. She seemed to understand him in a way that no one else did. Jerry believed he had finally connected with the love of his life, and their courtship progressed quickly to the marriage altar. Imagine the heartbreak

Jerry felt when he discovered that the warm, generous Linda he had courted was only a veneer to cover up an extremely self-centered Linda. Her needs were the only ones that mattered, and if Jerry didn't anticipate and gratify her wishes, she would pout, sulk, and throw temper tantrums.

For years, Jerry did his best to keep the peace—believing, as a Christian, he had no other alternative. In essence, Jerry capitulated to Linda. She ruled their home through icy indifference and stormy explosions. Jerry prayed for her and tried to reason with her, rewarding her tantrums with kindness and her demands with compliance. He believed that patience and gentleness would win her heart. He understood that she had grown up in a home with little love, and gave her lots of room to change. Meanwhile, Linda became only more confirmed in her selfishness. She had a predetermined heart.

In desperation, Jerry turned to God for other solutions. As he explored the life of Jesus, he saw that Jesus used firmness as well as gentleness in His dealings with individuals. He began to understand the games that the predetermined heart plays and principled options for breaking this cycle. He started to understand that true love is a proper balance of justice as well as mercy.

After much careful reflection and anguished prayer, he approached Linda. "Sweetheart, we can't go on like this. Your highs are too few, and your lows are too long and unpredictable. You keep me on a yo-yo, and it is going to have to stop. As I see it, we have five alternatives." Jerry showed her a slip of paper on which he had written the options as he saw them:

1. Remain as we are.
2. Seek counseling and actively apply it to both of our lives.
3. Set firmer boundaries with consequences if they are not met.
4. Separate.
5. Get a divorce.

Jerry continued, "In my opinion, the first and last options are neither biblical nor acceptable. My first choice would be to pursue number two, but I will respect your choice. Would you like counseling, firmer boundaries, or separation?"

Linda began to cry. "I don't want to lose you, Jerry. I'd rather fix what we have. Let's get counseling."

Jerry allowed her to choose the counselor, and she chose Sally and me. We had room for them in our schedule at that time, so we began to counsel with Jerry and Linda on a weekly basis. Linda had heard some of our messages about removing the thorns from a marriage, and she came to our first session fully armed with the thorns she wanted Jerry to remove.

"Lord," I prayed, "is 'removing the thorns' the right approach in this situation?"

"No, Jim. In this case, a different approach would be better."

"Jerry and Linda," I began, "let's restore love to your marriage. Let's bring back joy to your home. Here is the plan: Each of you should do all those things that made the other happy in the beginning of your relationship and stop doing all the things that have hurt each other since then. After that is in place, we will begin to address the thorns."

Jerry responded enthusiastically and was ready to get started. Linda became very quiet, very resistant, and very sulky. After much persuasion, she agreed to write down three things she wanted Jerry to do that would make her feel loved and to accept a similar list from Jerry. Later, after the counseling session, Jerry told us that Linda treated our assignment as if she had been asked to eat some putrid, decaying, dead thing. And in spite of her agreement, she did not follow through. If anything, her bad behavior worsened, and the tension in the home increased. Jerry did his best to follow through, but it was like trying to build a sand castle while his partner was busy tearing it down.

After several months of weekly counseling and trying different approaches, Jerry faced the fact that Linda had a predetermined heart. She would say with her lips that she wanted their marriage to work and that she was willing to do anything to bring that about, but her consistent failure to follow through with any plan to repair their damaged relationship and reignite love disproved the genuineness of her words.

Jerry moved to the next option he had to work with—more definite boundaries. Linda once again cried, and Jerry was moved to sympathy. But no change occurred. Instead, the tension heightened even further. In spite of all of Linda's tears and promises, she would not make the smallest change in her demeanor and deportment in the home. Not once did I see Linda follow through with any plan we recommended. That is one of the traits of the predetermined heart—saying, but not doing.

After nearly two years of working to save his marriage, Jerry had to face the hard reality that Linda had a predetermined heart and was not truly interested in changing. She wanted to continue the old manipulation and nonresolution and keep Jerry always off balance and struggling to maintain the peace. As a last resort, Jerry initiated a separation.

Once predetermined—always predetermined?

There is a spectrum—a continuum, if you will—between the two extremes of the predetermined heart and the listening heart. Not all those with predetermined hearts are beyond recovery. In the end, I believe we will be surprised who lines up on each side. Some we just knew had listening hearts, settle into being predetermined. Others whom we wrote off as unreachable, may in time prove to be among the most loyal. Why? Because beneath the hard crust of a predetermined heart, a listening heart can lie smoldering, just waiting for the right spark of conviction to ignite it into a brightly burning fire of love. How can we know? Apart from God, we can't!

Consider Saul of Tarsus who became Paul the missionary. Saul was fixed, determined, and stubborn. He persecuted the infant Christian church like a bulldog attacks a bone. When God, in a vision, told Ananias to go and minister to Saul of Tarsus that he might receive his sight, Ananias was incredulous! "Lord, are You sure You know what You're asking me to do? This man has a predetermined heart, if anyone ever did. Wouldn't I be playing right into his hands?"[23]

But God discerned a listening heart within Saul. He who reads the heart knows when we should "let them alone" and when it's time to knock on the door, looking for a listening heart just waiting to be drawn out. How do we know when this change occurs? By always maintaining a listening heart ourselves.

How do we knock? Like Jesus did. With a courageous conversation!

---

23. See Acts 9:10–18.

Chapter 4

A Predetermined Heart
Questions to Consider for Personal Inventory or Group Discussions

1. Do you have a predetermined heart when dealing with those who see things differently?
2. Do you possess a listening heart? A willingness to hear out the other side honestly and without bias?
3. Do you cater to policy, power, and position? Or do you follow principle?
4. Do you pursue hearts or ego and influence?
5. Are you able to forgive your tormentors?
6. Which thief on the cross best represents your experience?
7. Do you see some things so confidently that there is no room for possibly viewing them differently?
8. Are you biased, stubborn, and bullheaded?
9. Will you ask those who know you best which side of the chart on page 51 best describes you?
10. What would you have done with the woman who was caught in adultery? Stoned her? Or drawn out her heart?
11. Are you more interested in promoting your religion or in reaching lost souls?
12. Are you a lot like Sam? Linda?
13. Do you often "say" but not "do"?

Courageous Conversations

"If your brother wrongs you, go and have it out with him at once—just between the two of you. If he will listen to you, you have won him back as your brother."
—*Matthew 18:15, Phillips.*

"Saul, Saul, why persecutest thou me? And he said, Who art thou, Lord? And the Lord said, I am Jesus whom thou persecutest: it is hard for thee to kick against the pricks. And he trembling and astonished said, Lord, what wilt thou have me to do?"[1]

Now that's a courageous conversation! Of all the Jews, Saul had become the most determined persecutor of Jesus' disciples. Not content to harass them only in his backyard, he pursued them to Damascus with authorizing letters from the hierarchy of God's denominated church.

But God knew something about Saul that no one else did. Underneath the tough exterior of the proud Pharisee was a tender conscience. Witnessing Stephen's conduct at his trial and execution had sent a sharp arrow of conviction that pierced Saul's most sensitive spot. His attempts to ignore his conscience felt like kicking against the "pricks." God saw his struggle. He knew a ray of light had reached his heart. In spite of Saul's actions, regardless of what reason and common sense might dictate, Jesus confronted him.

That is the biblical principle. " 'If your brother wrongs you, go and

---

1. Acts 9:4–6.

have it out with him at once—just between the two of you. If he will listen to you, you have won him back as your brother.' "[2]

Notice the scripture doesn't say, "Go if you feel like it" or "Go if you have the verbal skills" or "Go if you are sure he'll hear you." Neither does it say, "Discuss it with someone else" or "Report it to others." It just says, "Go . . . at once . . . just between the two of you."

But that's hard! It's not comfortable! Don't you feel the excuses rising within you?

- "I'm not capable of pulling that off!"
- "What would I say?"
- "I'd be misunderstood."
- "I'd be too vulnerable. He'd see me as weak and petty and out maneuver me."
- "He'd reject me."
- "I'm scared; I don't want to!"

But God may have already pricked your brother's conscience. Most likely, he already knows in his heart what the issue is, and God wants to use you as His instrument to make wrongs right. Go ahead. Yield your fear to God. Pick up the phone. Write him a letter. Send an e-mail. Invite him over to your house or go out to eat. God is calling you to initiate a courageous conversation.

Base camp *first—then* the front lines

"He said what? Are you sure?" I was both shocked and wounded. "You're the second person who has shared that with me."

"What are you going to do?" Larry asked.

"I need to call him. May I use your name when I talk with him?"

"Yes, go ahead."

A short time later I found myself dialing Jeff's number. Jeff and I had been friends for a number of years and had worked on a couple of projects together. We worked well as a team, and I trusted him in spite of the fact that we disagreed strongly on one major area. I believe in what I call "base camp *first—then* front lines." Jeff believed in what he would call "front lines *now*."

---

2. Matthew 18:15, Phillips.

I believe that if you don't know how to swim, you don't go out as a lifeguard. If you can't swim, how on earth are you going to save those who are drowning? Reading a book about lifeguarding and becoming knowledgeable about the techniques don't give you the practical skill to rescue a drowning victim. It makes no difference that there are thousands of people drowning. You still must learn to swim and demonstrate that you know how to save those nearest you before you are ready to be a lifeguard. Otherwise, all you can do is offer those who are drowning academic information while they continue to flounder and sink beneath the waters of their sin.

That's what the base camp is all about. It's learning to apply the gospel in the most basic of duties and relationships. When you begin to abide in Christ amidst the trials and temptations that arise behind closed doors, you are beginning to swim. When you learn faithfulness in the duties that no one else sees, your swimming skills are strengthening. When you learn how to connect your family members to the same God who empowers you to swim, you are almost qualified to be a lifeguard. When your base camp is in order, then you are prepared for the front lines. Jeff likes to think you can secure your base camp while at the same time actively working the front lines. But what usually happens is that the front lines become so all-absorbing that the needs of the base camp are crowded out and its deficiencies are overlooked for a more promising work.

Jeff and I didn't agree. He had a burden to reach those in Africa who had never heard the name of Jesus. He wanted me to encourage everyone—regardless of his or her spiritual condition—to go and attempt to save the perishing before it was too late. I didn't believe I should use my influence to unreservedly encourage everyone to drop everything and go. Jeff's "go" is unqualified; mine is a qualified "go." Didn't Jesus say, "Tarry ye . . . until ye be endued with power from on high"?[3]

Have we found that power outside of us that enables us to live above our hereditary and cultivated tendencies to evil? Would our spouse say that we are truly born again? Have we raised up children who know how to walk with God in their daily lives? Isn't this the power that Jesus

---

3. Luke 24:49.

is referring to when He tells us to wait until we have power from on high? A power that transforms not only our mental beliefs but also our daily hour-by-hour choices? Jeff had told me that this was too discouraging. But isn't this the gospel that saves? If it doesn't save my marriage, my family, and me on a practical level, how on earth can I share anything that will save anyone else? I can't!

Regardless of whether you agree with Jeff or with me, that wasn't the issue to be discussed. The issue was what to do with someone who sees things differently from the way we do. This says more about the gospel we possess—or don't possess—than does all the truth we disagree over. So I found myself calling Jeff—not to discuss once again "base camp first, then front lines"—but rather to try to stop the innuendos, the undermining, and the insinuations before they turned into a mini-war.

A courageous conversation

"Jeff, this is Jim. I need to clear my slate with you. I know I'm catching you by surprise, so after I share my concerns with you, may I call you back in a few days after you have thought about them?"

Approach and attitude in a courageous conversation is of the greatest importance. If the other person senses that you are out for blood or intend to back him into a corner, you're better off ending the discussion right there. Deal with your own heart until the Holy Spirit subdues your disposition, and you can win your brother rather than reprove and rebuke him. This is paramount to removing the offense and saving the relationship. It's not a guarantee, but it definitely increases the odds for reconciliation.

"Go ahead, Jim," Jeff replied. "I don't think you'll need to call me back. What's on your mind?"

"Two friends have separately shared with me belittling comments you've been making toward me and my thoughts about securing base camp first before going to the front lines. They have also shared that you feel called to correct this supposed imbalance."

"Yes, I'd say that summarizes my position quite well. In fact, I'm surprised you haven't called me sooner. I've expected you to."

"Jeff, I'm not calling to do round four, five, or six again. We each have our perspectives, and we need to give each other the liberty to follow his own conscience. I'm calling to see if we can stop the guerrilla warfare occurring between us. I can allow you your perspective without attacking you or discrediting you to others. If your perspective is of God, it will bear fruit in the end. All I ask is that we each go about the work we feel God has called us to do without saying anything of a critical nature regarding each other. We have enough to do fighting the enemy without making each other out as the enemy. If God is with both you *and* me, that will show in the end too. I can be your friend and allow you room to see issues differently from the way I do and, in time, if we both follow God, He will balance us without us trying to take each other out."

"Jim, I want to apologize. You did the right thing calling. In fact, I feel relieved."

That's a summary of our conversation. In actuality, it took about an hour and a half. We each shared, laughed, and apologized. Each had the liberty to clear the slate entirely. We managed to remove the thorn before it divided the relationship. In fact, the friendship is stronger as a result. Yours can be, too, if someone will risk a courageous conversation.

If you're that one, then go to God. Let Him humble you and put a listening heart into you. Go with His Spirit of reconciliation and a forgiving heart—as well as with the facts as you understand them. Don't go to reprove or for blood. Go to open up a listening heart.

A science to be mastered

The underlying purpose of a courageous conversation is not to score points or vent your feelings. It is to rebuild a relationship, to heal and repair—not to inflict further damage. There is a science to restoring relationships, and that science encompasses discipline, knowledge, tact, and heart.

If we have been hurt, injured, or wronged, it requires discipline to follow the biblical principle, "Tell him his fault between thee and him alone."[4] It requires discipline not to spread your side of the story to other sympathetic ears. It requires discipline to forgive the other party in your heart even before he has asked for forgiveness. It requires discipline not to run and hide, capitulate, or fight back. How is this discipline

---

4. Matthew 18:15.

gained? By gritting your teeth? No! It is gained through a daily abiding experience in Jesus.

The hurt and injury we have inflicted upon God far outstrip anything our associates may have done to us. We have snubbed our Maker and Redeemer, ignored Him, dishonored Him, and shamed Him—often without recognizing it, even when we claimed to be representing Him. And what does He do with us? Just as He did with Saul of Tarsus—He looks for an opportunity to confront us with the reality of what we are doing. When we finally drop our defenses, He wraps His arms around us and makes us His partners. When we experience a walk with Him on a daily basis, we gain the essential knowledge needed to master the science of restoring relationships. As I cooperate with His restoration methods, I learn how to restore my relationships with others. And as I implement His teachings in my daily life, I gain tact in approaching my courageous conversations.

Tact is an essential element that we learn from Christ. It develops within us the skill of considering the other party's feelings and sensing what is right and appropriate in a given situation. It leads us to use discretion and not just dump our grievances on our brother. It helps us to speak with a meek and lowly spirit. "You who are spiritual restore such a one in a spirit of gentleness."[5] Being meek and lowly are *not* the same thing as being weak and groveling. It is recognizing—and bearing in mind continually—our indebtedness to God.

When we approach our brother realizing that he, too, has been bought with the blood of Christ, we will treat him as such. Harsh condemnation will be out of place. Conveying our "superiority" through our countenance, words, or gestures will be avoided. We won't compare our goodness or supposed righteousness with his failings. Tact will be aware of any approach that includes disdain, contempt, or an overbearing spirit. It will avoid every appearance of anger, hate, ill will, bitterness, or sour expression. And yet, it will be honest, forthright, and frank. It will not beat around the bush and leave the other person wondering what we are really talking about.

This science to be mastered is from the heart and must, therefore, be preceded by personal heart work. Go before God to examine your own

---

5. Galatians 6:1, NKJV.

motives and purposes. Ask for His input on your approach, because the approach must be balanced—balanced by a sensitivity to how God has dealt with us and how He would have us deal with the other party in combination with the desire to restore the broken relationship.

You can speak so gently and softly that you never get to the facts or the difficulty at hand, and the other person fails to comprehend the situation you are confronting. Or you can so overstate your case, beating him to death with your hurt and injury, that the other party shuts down. Either imbalance will cause you to fail to reach your goal.

We should speak in a serious, plain, solemn manner because relationships, God's work, and the salvation of souls are at stake. We need to clear our slates of all that hinders us from a true-hearted commitment to loving the brethren. We should be honest yet kind, truthful yet compassionate, forthright yet still diplomatic. Facts, truth, and an honest, heartfelt perspective entered into with much prayer and a humble, entreating spirit can go a long way in bridging the abyss.

Two common sins

Two sins are common to us all—the sin of *omission* and the sin of *commission*. One usually follows the other.

The sin of omission is avoiding the courageous conversation. It is failing to tell our brother his fault and to share our grievances. It's much easier to avoid the vulnerability that comes with face-to-face confrontation. It's so easy to find excuses not to do it. It's so easy, in fact, that it has become the norm. The problem is human nature just loves to express itself. It longs for sympathy and understanding, and, too often, that leads to the sin of commission.

The sin of commission is publishing your brother's faults and failures to another person or persons. So often we claim we are just getting another person's perspective or some good counsel and advice. Or we say, "You need to pray for so and so because . . . because . . . because!" Or we just out-and-out cannibalize our brother's character, winning adherents to ourselves and teaching our brother a lesson. But God sees through all these actions.

Before Calvary, Jesus never revealed to the other disciples that Judas was embezzling funds. Why?

Neither should we neglect our duty of going to our brother just because it's a hard thing to do or because we tell ourselves, "I'm just not able to do it." God set up no criteria for backing out of courageous conversations.

I believe that the sin of commission customarily follows the sin of omission. When the hurt we feel and the injustice we see continues building in our thoughts and emotions, there comes a time when we "have to" let it out. Unfortunately, when we resist taking it directly to the one in the wrong, we spread it like the leaves of autumn to all we come in contact with. Thus, we become guilty first of the sin of omission and then of the sin of commission.

All our efforts to rectify the wrongs we see may avail nothing. Our brother may repay us evil for good. He may be enraged rather than convinced. He may hear to no good purpose and continue to pursue the evil course he is on. If so, treat him kindly and leave him for your heavenly Father to deal with.

In some cases, further action may be warranted. Then Jesus instructs us to approach our brother again—this time with one or two additional individuals. If that attempt fails in situations where discipline is needed, we are to take the matter before the church[6]—remembering that the *motive* for discipline is *love* and the *purpose* is to *restore*.

Unfortunately, however, in the vast majority of cases, the courageous conversation is omitted, is carried out in an alienating manner, or is approached only after we have told everyone else. Let this not be said of us!

It's scary!

Over the years I have noticed many friendships fall by the wayside for lack of openhearted, in-depth conversation. This was happening with two friends of mine, so I strongly encouraged them to have a courageous conversation with each other. See if you can enter into their situation. Some of the details may vary from the situation you may be facing, but the solution may still work for you.

Today was the day! Erica and I were to have a courageous conversation with Joe and Lisa, and we were shaking in our boots. It shouldn't have been that way. We had been friends for

---

6. See Matthew 18:16, 17.

more than twenty years. Joe and I had been college buddies, had married our girlfriends about the same time, settled in the same small town, attended the same church, and started our families at about the same time. Our children attended school together. We planned our vacations together. Whenever possible, we celebrated Thanksgiving and Christmas together. It was obvious to everyone that we were the best of friends—just like family, in fact!

But something had happened that changed all that. One of our family vacations included attending a family camp meeting that featured the Hohnbergers. As we listened to their intensely practical messages on the Christian life, we each were convicted that we needed to simplify our lives, reorder our priorities, and schedule our time better. We went home to do just that—and that's when things started changing between us. Seems rather strange, doesn't it? I mean, when you move closer to God, don't you automatically move closer to one another?

In time both of our families moved to quiet country locations—but in different directions. We no longer attended the same church, and our children no longer attended the same school. We didn't think these changes would affect our friendship, but they did.

Over the next two years, we noted somewhat sadly that the closeness between us was dwindling. We usually saw each other at group functions and greeted each other warmly, but something was missing. It didn't occur to us that maybe Joe and Lisa sensed the same thing or that we could talk about it. At one of these occasions, I noticed Joe and Lisa deeply engaged in conversation with Alex and Sharon, who had recently moved to the area. They seemed to be really hitting it off.

A few days later, Erica and I heard through mutual friends that Joe and Lisa were in a real bind to complete a project they were engaged in as a family business and that they needed help. We called them and offered to spend our family day helping them. When we arrived at their place, we were surprised to see Alex, Sharon, and their children already there. "Well, the more the merrier," we told each other.

But as the day progressed, it became evident that Joe and Lisa were very taken with their new friends. The four of them chatted nonstop and hardly seemed to notice or care that Erica and I were on the sidelines. We ended that day with the sinking feeling that our friendship simply was no longer a priority to Joe and Lisa. While it bothered us, it didn't seem to bother them.

Pushing aside our hurt, we continued to make needed changes in our own family and, in the process, found new friends. We saw Joe and Lisa from time to time, but there was a growing coolness between us, and we assumed they wanted it that way. We buried our hurt within our hearts and accepted things as they seemed to be.

Our friendship would probably have died a natural death if Jim had not urged both of us to have a courageous conversation. I thought he was crazy. Talking *to* them about our feelings *about* them would be way too vulnerable. No way! But Jim presented his case for Matthew 18 and courageous conversations so persuasively that we agreed to pray about it. And as we did so, the conviction deepened in us that we should approach our friends, but they beat us to it.

"Hey, Todd," Joe stammered over the phone, "you know how Jim has been trying to get us to talk to each other about . . . uh . . . er . . . well . . . you know. I was wondering, would you and Erica be willing to come over for dinner next Tuesday night, and we could . . . uh . . . talk?"

I took a deep breath. My mouth suddenly seemed stuffed with cotton balls. I coughed, swallowed hard, and then answered. "Thanks for calling, Joe. We'll be happy to accept."

As we thought about what we would say, it became more and more difficult to actually come up with anything that we could point to as a cause of our diminishing friendship. It had just slipped away and didn't seem to matter. What would we say? Then we became somewhat afraid of what Joe and Lisa would have to say about what we might have done that would have caused them to think that we didn't want to be close to them anymore.

The day of the meeting arrived and with it came anxiety. Our thoughts ran in many different directions. We began to wonder if the friendship was really worth the risk. We never had to do this before, and it felt so awkward and uncomfortable.

But as we prayed, we realized this is what we have to do in our marriage. We don't just throw away our marriage because it requires work or because we don't always agree on everything. We work at keeping it alive.

Another thought that awakened in us the desire to go through with this courageous conversation was the idea that we had nothing to lose and much to gain. By facing this uncomfortable conversation, we would have an opportunity to see and correct mistakes we had made and thereby strengthen our own characters. And, we might win back our friendship. Even if the conversation failed to bring us back together, we would lose it anyway if we continued in the same old path.

As we drove to their house, a jumble of thoughts paraded through my mind. *What are they going to say? Have I done something to offend them? Have I hurt them? Have we just grown apart? Do they want to continue the friendship?*

We had dinner together, and then the children went off to play. The four of us sort of stood around in the kitchen just chatting, wondering who would have the courage to start the courageous conversation.

Joe finally broke the ice and got to the point of our meeting. "Why don't you two want to be friends with us anymore?" he blurted out.

"What?" I replied incredulously. "We never stopped wanting to be your friends. We thought you didn't want our friendship anymore."

"That never entered our minds!" Joe exclaimed. "We saw you guys progressing so well in your family's experience that we didn't think we were good enough for you anymore. And then you started hanging out with the Smiths and getting along so well with them . . . and well . . . we just let it go."

"But what about your friendship with Alex and Sharon?" I countered. "You guys seemed so chummy—we just assumed you were moving on with your own lives."

As we shared freely, we discovered that neither of us had anything major on our slates. Our friendship had been the near victim of neglect and misunderstanding. Little looks misinterpreted. Little attentions lacking. Little comments misconstrued. All these things were small molehills in reality. But because we had been too cowardly to confront them, they had turned into mountains between us.

After all was said and done, the four of us understood that our friendship was irreplaceable and that we truly love each other. We realized that keeping a friendship alive and growing takes more than playing and having fun together in a group. It takes individual time to talk one-on-one. It takes honesty and vulnerability. And at times, it takes a courageous conversation.

This relationship was not only restored but also enhanced because both sides were willing to risk an awkward, true-hearted, and honest sharing. Yours could be next! Is God asking you to do something similar? If so, the names and concerns are already in your thoughts. Go ahead and call them before you get distracted or talk yourself out of it.

Jesus makes it clear that when He asks us to initiate courageous conversations we may or may not find a happy ending. How many of those in whom He sought to awaken a listening heart spurned Him? How many sneered at His best efforts? How many shoved His love and concern back in His face? Have you? Have I? And yet, He continues to lead us along the higher road. Will we follow Him?

Rejection

Albert belonged to a group with a strong emphasis on practical religion. The members shared each others' joys and sorrows. The greatest interest of their leader, Phillip, was to help them be successful in their Christian walk. Albert had been a part of the group for many years and played an active role. He and Sam, the assistant leader, were very close friends. They openly shared their views and discussed their ideas with each other. More than that, they felt comfortable opening their hearts to one another, encouraging and helping each other. Sam had said of Albert, "He is my best friend in America."

But over the years, a change gradually took place. The group's lively interest in practical religion was replaced with an emphasis on doctrine. A zeal for correct scriptural exposition replaced their willingness to face and overcome character deficiencies. In time, it became evident why that change took place. Phillip, the leader, had drawn a circle to define his life—and that circle excluded his wife. The first time he was unfaithful to her, he responded to the promptings of his wounded conscience and openly confessed and put away his sin. Unfortunately, he gave way to the temptation again, and this time he did not confess until he was found out. The fallout of this sad story was that Phillip left the group—but not before he introduced a controversial new teaching that became generally accepted by most of the members of the group.

Albert carefully studied the subject and became convinced that the teaching was based on a faulty premise. Confident that his brethren were open-minded, he approached Sam to suggest a courageous conversation.

"You know, Sam," Albert began, "I'm concerned about this new idea Phillip has introduced. Most of the people in our group seem to have accepted it, but my study has raised some real questions in my mind. I'm concerned about where this might lead. I'd like to suggest that we have an open meeting to discuss this issue."

Sam reluctantly agreed to plan a meeting but never settled on a date and time. Weeks dragged by and turned into months. Still Sam didn't schedule a meeting. Albert began to conclude that the meeting would never take place.

Albert continued to attend meetings regularly and to fellowship with the group, but something was changing. No one—not even the other leaders—were willing to discuss or study Albert's concerns with him, even on an informal basis. They treated him kindly, but he got the distinct impression that they distrusted him and were trying to love him back into conformity with their thinking.

How long this state of affairs would have continued is unknown, but then Tony and Dan, close friends of the group, arrived for a special Week of Prayer and became aware of the situation. They insisted at once upon holding a meeting to deal with the situation.

"Albert," Sam told him abruptly, "we're going to have that meeting you've been wanting. Tony and Dan will be there, along with the group leaders—about ten of us. We'd like to hear your concerns."

"Certainly," Albert replied. "When would you like to meet?"

"At five-thirty tonight."

Albert glanced at his watch. "But that's just an hour from now. I really could use a little more time to prepare a good presentation. Is there any chance we could schedule the meeting for tomorrow right before the morning meeting?"

"No. This is the only time available. Take it or leave it."

As Albert considered his reply, he looked into Sam's eyes. This was the man who, at one time, had called him his "best friend in America." Why the unbending attitude? Why the hard look? Why the long delay and then the sudden demand for an immediate meeting?

"Sure, Sam," Albert said. "I'll be there."

In spite of his leadership role within the group, Albert had a deeply entrenched fear of public speaking. Having to face the group on such short notice and feeling unprepared triggered his anxiety. Sure, he had studied and knew his subject well, but to present it under these circumstances seemed an overwhelming task.

As Albert entered the conference room an hour later, he sensed a distance on the part of the others. He noted their frowns and whispers. No one greeted him. The chairman began the meeting by reminding everyone that they had one hour to resolve this issue and urged Albert to be succinct in his presentation.

Albert swallowed hard and began. Doing his best to yield his uneasiness to God, he outlined his objections to the doctrine under question. However, he quickly realized that this was not an open forum for investigation; rather, his listeners had predetermined opinions that they were determined to protect at all costs. They tried with their utmost to convince him to agree with them. When he said that he could not agree with them on this point, they told him that he could no longer preach to the group. They could find no charge against his character and agreed that he was in harmony with the gospel and all the fundamental doctrines—except this new teaching.

Albert left that meeting with powerful emotions surging through him. He had the assurance of honest convictions and the evidence for his convictions, yet he was not only facing a storm without, but also a storm within. He was disappointed that he had not been able to examine the evidence calmly with openhearted brethren.

Albert continued to worship with this group for another year, hoping and wishing for a change of heart. He finally had to face the fact that their hearts were closed. He had attempted to have a courageous conversation, and it had failed to restore the relationship. He had remained open to dialogue and discussion for a long time, but they were closed.

Albert was crushed, disappointed, and confused. How could this be? How could this happen? Where would he go now? What would he do? As he wrestled through the failure of his courageous conversation, he recognized something new. He realized that he *needed* God—needed Him *desperately*. Why? Because he was facing rejection. And he had no defense for rejection!

CHAPTER 5

COURAGEOUS CONVERSATIONS

Questions to Consider for Personal Inventory or Group Discussions

1. Are you willing to have a courageous conversation with the "Sauls" in your life?
2. When someone wrongs you, do you follow the counsel of Matthew 18:15?
3. How many courageous conversations have you initiated in your life?
4. Would you have called Jeff? If no, why not?
5. In a courageous conversation, what is your approach and attitude with someone who disagrees with you?
6. Can you allow someone to have a differing perspective without setting off a mini-war?
7. Can you apologize when you see you've been wrong?
8. Are you guilty of the sin of omission? Of the sin of commission?
9. In the quietness of your conscience, what is God calling you to do?
10. Have you ever had to face rejection by those close to you? How did you respond?

The Walking Wounded

They sing the song of Moses . . . and the song of the Lamb.
—Revelation 15:3

"Sometimes I wish I'd never had children!"

The words sliced into four-year-old Albert like shrapnel. Bad weather had cooped up him and his four siblings inside a small house. They played hide-and-seek, horsey, and ring-around-the-rosy—making the best of a dreary afternoon. Their mother, however, was struggling with trials her children didn't understand. She was tired and longed for quiet. Her nerves finally reached the breaking point, and she snapped out a thoughtless jab. "Why can't you kids be quiet? Sometimes I wish I'd never had children!"

Albert felt like his world was crumbling around him. His siblings went on playing, but he was reduced to tears in the corner of the living room. His uncontrolled sobs eventually drew the attention of his distraught mother.

"Albert," she chided, "what's wrong with you? Why are you crying?"

Between his sobs, Albert choked out, "Because . . . you wish . . . you didn't have . . . me!"

"Oh, Albert, I didn't really mean that. Mama's just tired—that's all."

But the message had already been driven into Albert's heart like a sharp splinter into tender flesh: *When I don't meet the expectations of those I love, they will reject me.* His mother brushed away his tears and figured he'd forget about it. Life went on.

Albert did get over it—outwardly at least. But the message buried deep in his subconscious remained like an embedded splinter. Albert had joined the league of the walking wounded.

Casualties of war and life

The walking wounded—these are the casualties of war, terrorism, or disaster who are able to walk despite their injuries. In wartime, the treatment of their wounds takes lowest priority. Likewise, there are the walking wounded who are casualties of *life*—wounded by words, looks, and acts of insensitivity. These wounds to the spirit are invisible to the eye, and most of them go untreated.

Planet Earth is a war zone. Every child of Adam, born to reflect God's image, is a target for the archenemy who first launched his missiles in heaven. Few of us pass through this world unscathed by his tactics, and Christians are the special subjects of his attacks. We become the walking wounded when conservatives attack liberals and liberals attack conservatives. I see it everywhere I go—Christians wounding Christians in mini-wars in our churches, friendships, and, saddest of all, in our families.

Albert's mother had no intention of driving the splinter of rejection into her child. But Albert's enemy did. As a child, Albert was defenseless. Children build their sense of reality on what is presented to them. They don't have the ability to recognize subtleties for what they really are, and the splinter goes in. Just as our physical bodies attempt to "wall off" a splinter, so our minds build protective shields around emotional splinters. These wounds—like festering abscesses—may be tucked away out of sight, but they are still there. They still cause pain. They still deform the image of God in that person. Until the splinter is removed—the subtle innuendo replaced with truth—there will be no true healing.

The problem is that we are so skilled at concealing the splinters and accepting them as an integral part of ourselves that often we don't even realize we are wounded. God will not force surgery upon us to remove the splinter. While waiting for our cooperation, He tries to call our attention to the offending splinter: He allows it to be bumped. He allows circumstances to arise that penetrate the shields we have built-up and prick that most sensitive spot. He allows us to feel our helplessness until we realize our need of Him.

Choices

In Albert's case, the failure of his attempted courageous conversation with Sam and the other group leaders echoed the same message he had heard and believed when he was four years old—a message he had embraced throughout his life: *When I'm different, I'm rejected. When I don't measure up, I'll be ostracized.* Now, nearing his retirement years, Albert again came face to face with that same old lie. He couldn't escape the throbbing of that splinter of rejection—and he didn't know how to remove it.

Albert had five choices:

1. Deny that the splinter exists.
2. Continue to live with the splinter.
3. Lash out at those who bump the splinter.
4. Withdraw into self-protective isolation.
5. Turn to the Great Physician, and let Him remove the splinter.

Many choose to deny that the splinter exists and do whatever it takes to medicate or dull the pain it produces. They bury themselves in business ventures, hobbies, or even religious activities. Others live a vicarious existence through the entertainment world. Still others resort to substance abuse or sexual indulgence. But the pain remains—throbbing every time the mind quiets down enough to engage the inner reality.

Others don't deny the problem, but they prefer to endure it. They mistakenly think that having it removed would take too much effort and cause too much pain. So they build their protective shields stronger and thicker around the splinter. The energy they could direct toward seeking God for healing they misdirect into protecting their inner hurt. They may seem fine outwardly—superficially—but the splinter causes an abscess to form, and the wound enlarges beneath the surface like a hidden cancer.

The third option—lashing out at those who are bumping the painful spot—often kicks in when the first two don't work well. It's called "an eye for an eye." You hurt me, so my fleshly response is to spread gossip, assassinate your character, and misrepresent you. Remember the well-known Hatfields and McCoys—two families in the Appalachian Mountains who carried on feuds and vengeance for generations? The devil revels in this kind of warfare, especially in God's remnant church.

The fourth option is the opposite of the third—withdrawing, avoiding courageous conversations, and crawling into a self-protective shell so you don't have to face your own inadequacies or their manipulative justifications. It may seem comfortable for a while, but it never heals the wound.

Finally, the last option is what we all need and what God desires for us—healing. None of us can escape being wounded, but we don't need to remain wounded. God wants to do far more for us than just help us cope with our wounds; He wants to heal them. In Him, we can rise above them.

None of us can escape being wounded. But it's what we do with the wounds that really matters. Jesus was wounded again and again, but He didn't succumb to His wounds. Instead, He learned from His suffering.[1] He showed us that what counts is not how we are wounded but how we handle our wounds. We can learn to find peace in the midst of our wounding.

Many of these walking wounded are among us today. Often the wounds begin when we are young and continue into the adult years. However, not everyone who sees themselves as having been wounded by frenemy fire actually has been. Some—like Lena and Toby—are wounded while in their young, tender years, but also inflict wounds on themselves.

False martyrdom

There are certainly false martyrs in our ranks. Lena was an unusually talented and attractive woman who seemed to have more than her share of disappointments in life. She appeared to be a constant target for what she considered to be frenemy fire, and, naturally, she found this very painful. Friendship after friendship floundered and fizzled. Job after job soured. Her marriage ended in divorce.

As Lena recounted her saga to us, one thing became apparent: Each failed relationship was always the fault of the other party—never Lena's

---

1. See Hebrews 5:8.

fault. Never. Either the other party ended the relationship, or they behaved in such ways that Lena was forced to end it. Lena always felt like the helpless victim of uncaring people—another of the walking wounded.

Sally and I wondered if Lena's view was really the whole picture. We suspected it was not, and further discussions revealed we were correct. Much of what Lena called frenemy fire was self-induced. Lena had some major splinters she was protecting—splinters that God wanted to turn into stepping-stones. Raised by an overly sweet, yet domineering mother and a father who fluctuated between indulging and terrorizing his family, Lena had learned that "I'm happy when someone is giving me just what I want, and I'm miserable when they're not." In addition, she had never learned the difference between loving confrontation and hurtful criticism.

Lena always began a new friendship enthusiastically. This new friend was the one she had been looking for all her life. This new friend would never abandon her. This new friend would never let her down as all the others had. She would throw herself into the new relationship, almost to the exclusion of previous friendships, and at first, everything would go well. Lena would be happy. Inevitably, though, the new friend would cross Lena—perhaps unintentionally—and Lena would pout. Or the new friend might need a little breathing room—and Lena would panic. Eventually, the new friend might confront Lena's manipulative behavior—and Lena would cry, "Frenemy fire!" It seemed as though she couldn't handle a fly landing on her nose.

Was Lena really experiencing frenemy fire? No. What she saw as attacks by her friends were honest concerns for her character and desires to improve their relationship. The problem was that Lena could not look honestly at herself for fear that part of the problem might truly be her responsibility. That would inflame her emotional splinter of rejection. Therefore, Lena was determined to deny responsibility and avoid it at all costs. Anyone who bumped her wound became a frenemy, and Lena played the part of the helpless victim. We all have varying degrees of Lena in us.

As a child, Lena may have been a victim of her family's inadequacies, but as an adult, she no longer needs to be a victim. God was giving her the opportunity to be the victor. How? By giving her chance after chance to recognize the splinter so that He could remove it for her. But she would not face it—anything but face it!

Terri was one friend who braved a courageous conversation with Lena, not to tear her down or to criticize her, but to share a genuine concern. They chatted pleasantly as they walked together through a quiet park. Sitting down on a bench, they paused. Terri sent up a prayer for guidance and then gently began. "Lena, I really value your friendship. You are fun to be with. You're enthusiastic about almost any adventure we get into. You have a very creative mind, and you challenge me in a lot of ways."

Lena listened quietly, watching the ducks paddle on the nearby pond.

Terri continued. "I have just one small concern. I wonder if you would be willing to hear me out and then consider it, letting God speak to you."

Lena shrugged her shoulders, avoided eye contact with Terri, and replied, "Sure, go ahead."

"I've noticed quite often that when things don't go the way you want, that you—how can I say this?—you sort of pout. You get real quiet, and when you do talk, it's mostly negative jabs about what you don't like. It just brings a real cloud over the day, and often I don't know what happened to make you act that way."

Lena buried her face in her hands and began sobbing. Terri put her arms around her. "Lena, I'm not saying this to hurt you. I know what it's like. I used to do the same thing. But God is helping me to learn that I can be happy even when things don't go my way."

Lena continued to weep—refusing to speak or to respond to Terri. Terri tried to console her, but Lena would not be consoled.

From that day on, Lena avoided Terri. She kept their telephone conversations brief and superficial. Terri would invite Lena to her home, but Lena always had other plans. Later, Lena told us that Terri had been very mean to her and that she couldn't afford to spend time with her anymore.

Lena suffered deeply, but her suffering did her no good. It was wasted, useless. All her suffering came about because she refused to face her splinter. She denied it, avoided it, shielded it, and lashed out at those who bumped it—all the while, claiming frenemy fire. The storm within made her think that she was facing a storm without, but it was self-induced. As long as she remained on this path of false martyrdom, she would never be able to sing the song of Moses and the Lamb—the song of triumph. She would remain the victim rather than the victor.

The same was true of Toby.

Toby's wife, Sarah, had just asked him to move out of their home; she wasn't willing to live with him any longer. Understandably, this was a blow that sent Toby reeling. He confided to me that he could really identify with what Joseph must have felt when he was sold into slavery by his brothers. Was this frenemy fire? Was Toby shot in the back? Were his wounds without cause? Or was he throwing up a protective shield because he refused to look honestly at himself?

Let me share a bit more of Toby's story.

The rest of the story

Toby was born into the brotherhood of the walking wounded. Conceived outside of marriage, he was born to a teenage mother who was overwhelmed with the daily tirades of anger displayed by her childish husband. As Toby grew, his parents placed few restrictions on him. He could come and go as he pleased with little accountability for his actions. His father's harsh verbal jabs and his mother's aloof indifference—together with the lack of structure and accountability in the home—communicated to Toby that he was not welcome or loved. He learned to equate self-indulgence with love and to believe that "my way is the only way."

As Toby entered his teen years, there was nothing to restrain him from engaging fully in the party scene with all the promiscuity and substance abuse that attends it. At the age of nineteen he married Mona, his pregnant girlfriend. Mona expected Toby's behavior would change once they were married and that she would be his only lover. However, Toby had never recognized restrictions before and saw no reason to start now.

After several turbulent years, Mona started cheating on Toby just as he had been cheating on her all along—and Toby was devastated. Mona told him that she had endured enough and wanted nothing more to do with him. He hit bottom and thought about ending his life. That's when God finally got Toby's attention.

A friend shared with him a little book, *Steps to Christ*. Toby took it home and read the entire book in one night. It convicted him that he was a sinner, that God loved him, and that he could be saved by grace. Falling on his knees, he sobbed out his repentance and begged God to accept him. Peace came into his soul for the first time in his life.

When Toby woke up the next morning, he knew his life was different. He had lost his taste for alcohol. Never again would he use marijuana, tobacco, or cocaine. He began to study the Bible with his Christian friend and was amazed at what he learned. He gave up partying and became a vegetarian. In time he was baptized. The change in his life was so remarkable that a number of people urged him to attend college and become a pastor.

No one told Toby that he still had splinters to deal with. No one taught Toby that God wants to take us through a process of removing the splinters and use them as stepping-stones for growth in the Christian walk. Toby honestly believed that all the issues in his past were taken care of and now all he needed to do to live a Christian life was to continue to believe and accept correct doctrinal and lifestyle issues and to witness to others.

Toby met Pam at a Christian college. After a whirlwind courtship, they got married—fully expecting bliss. But subconsciously, Toby still believed that marriage means "she gives everything and expects nothing, while I take everything and give only what I feel like giving." He had no clue that there is no love without sacrifice. The old splinter—"my way is the only way"—was still there. He expected to come and go as he pleased. He expected his wife to keep the home clean, prepare appetizing meals, wash and iron his clothes, and be an enthusiastic bed partner. And he expected her to require nothing of him in return beyond what he felt like giving. He expected her to respond with affection even if he was quiet, sour, and moody. He believed that a wife should submit to her husband, even when the husband is not submitting to God.

Pam was shocked and incensed. The Toby behind closed doors was so different from the Toby who had courted her at school. It wasn't that she didn't want to do all the things that Toby expected of her—it was just that she thought the relationship should be mutual, not one-sided. Toby couldn't understand her viewpoint. But instead of asking God what he should do differently, he withdrew more and more into sports and evangelism.

He encouraged Pam to go for counseling, thinking that everything would be just fine if a counselor were to straighten out Pam. She went and begged Toby to go with her. He refused. He didn't have a problem; she did. Toby believed that because he was now a Christian, heavily involved with church programs, and living a clean lifestyle, he was OK. He didn't need to look any deeper. He remained locked in denial.

When Pam finally separated from Toby and then filed for divorce, he was devastated once again. He felt misunderstood, misused, and persecuted. He thought he was the object of frenemy fire and endured his suffering in such a way that many of his friends viewed him as a sort of patient martyr. Their sympathy helped to shield Toby from actually admitting he had some splinters to remove.

No one told him that his suffering was the fruit of his own character problems and that he should see it as a wake-up call. God saw his scars and wanted to turn them into stars. But instead of facing his scars, Toby hid in denial. This is false martyrdom. It is wasted suffering. It could have been turned into a valuable experience if Toby had been willing to engage in the process of removing his splinters. Instead, he remained one of the walking wounded.

This kind of thing happens far too often. People face crises and suffering in their lives, and their friends support them in ways that do not make them face the growth steps they need to take to keep from repeating their mistakes. They see themselves as victims and set themselves up for failure all over again. As the Bible says, "As a dog returns to its vomit, so a fool repeats his folly."[2]

I met Toby as his third marriage was tottering. He was repeating the old familiar patterns and finding the same results with Sarah. Toby attended a number of our seminars, and we had some long talks.

"Jim, I'm doing the same thing to Sarah that I did to Mona and Pam. I can't bear the thought of losing a third marriage. What can I do?" Toby was no longer denying his splinters—neither was he shielding them.

"Toby," I counseled, "Your solution is simple. You must replace *'my way'* with *'Lord, what would You have me to do?'* You need to ask God to show you where your selfish focus arises and how to actively engage in

---

2. Proverbs 26:11, NIV.

replacing it with practical self-sacrifice for Sarah. You must ask yourself, 'How can I serve my wife?' instead of 'How can I manipulate my wife into serving me?' Instead of dwelling on what bugs you about Sarah, you must replace those negative thoughts with what you love about Sarah. Instead of coming home at night with a cold shoulder and a sour expression on your face, smile and enter into friendly conversation. Instead of demanding that your needs be met regardless of her day and her trials, look for little acts of service you can do cheerfully to communicate that you care for her. You must daily put God in charge of every thought you think, every word you speak, and every act you perform. If you will do this, your marriage will sparkle, and you will become Sarah's hero."

Toby was quiet and thoughtful. Then he made a commitment. "I'm going to do it, Jim. Sarah is worth it!" And he started out enthusiastically. Sarah responded with renewed hope.

But then Toby's old impulses rose up stronger than ever—and Toby gave in to them. He wouldn't follow through with his good intentions. He dropped the new program after only a few days, and things were worse than ever for months. Toby and Sarah would attend another meeting, and Toby would decide to try again. But he always tired of the effort and went back to the old ways—claiming that he didn't know what to do.

Sarah finally realized that Toby wasn't willing to give up his splinters. Neither was he willing to lay down his shield of irresponsibility. She asked Toby to move out.

Once again, Toby was devastated. That's when he shared with me that he could identify with Joseph being sold by his brothers into slavery. He felt that he was the object of his wife's frenemy fire. He played well the role of a martyr. He claimed he was being rejected. But this was a self-imposed rejection. Once again he surrounded himself with friends who sympathized with him but did not hold him accountable. At the time of this writing he has not found deliverance nor has he been able to sing the song of Moses and the Lamb.

It doesn't have to be that way. We can choose to leave the path of false martyrdom and enter the path of triumph. The following table summarizes the characteristics of both paths. As you study it, ask yourself, Where am I in this picture? Which path am I following? What is God laying on my heart right now?

The Walking Wounded

False Martyrdom	Path of Triumph
Reactive—ruled by inclination.	Proactive—ruled by godly principle.
Acts like a helpless victim; believes someone else is responsible to fix things.	Takes responsibility for finding healing even if initially a victim.
Labels all confrontation or input as frenemy fire.	Sorts out helpful input from "new splinters."
Protects wounds at all costs and expects others to do the same.	Identifies protective responses and yields them to God.
Believes problem are always caused by circumstances or other people—never by his own responses.	Believes that circumstances provide opportunities to learn better responses.
Sees the grace of God only as a means of coping with the splinter, not removing it.	Sees the grace of God as a means of removing the splinter and healing the wound.
Allows circumstances to master him.	Allows circumstances to become rungs on a ladder to gain a higher experience.
Engages in "poor me" pity parties.	Has an attitude of gratitude.
Claims, "I just don't know what to do."	Believes, "God will tell me the next step, and I will take it with my hand in His."
Becomes bitter.	Becomes better.
Remains emotionally unstable.	Becomes increasingly emotionally stable.
Shows characteristics of the predetermined heart.	Shows characteristics of a listening heart.
Nurtures a protective shield.	Deals with his imbalances.
Stays busy with activities that crowd out time for introspection.	Plans time with God to actively examine himself.
Surrounds himself with people who will protect his splinters.	Chooses companions who help him honestly face his splinters.

Embrace it

The only way to transform the suffering that comes from our splinters is to embrace it. We must face ourselves—our past and our present—with God. But that's hard! It doesn't come naturally! Our entire being rebels against it! We are a lot like Peter! Jesus was describing His future to the disciples—and it didn't fit their plans. (How often does suffering fit into our plans?) They expected to see Him conquer the Romans and rule the world with them as His top officials.

When Jesus told them that He would suffer and die instead, they all disliked the idea. Peter spoke up and told Jesus that there was no need for all that,[3] but Jesus sharply confronted him. " 'Get behind Me, Satan! You are an offense to Me, for you are not mindful of the things of God, but the things of men.' "[4]

Jesus didn't stop there. He drove the point home even more strongly. " 'If anyone would come after me, he must deny himself and take up his cross and follow me. For whoever wants to save his life will lose it, but whoever loses his life for me will find it.' "[5]

Jesus calls us to embrace suffering, not to avoid it. He says that we must forsake the pattern of protecting our splinters and instead put down our shields, pick up our crosses, and follow Him.

The lesson was not lost on Peter. Calvary brought him face to face with his splinter of self-preservation and his shield of self-sufficiency. Christ had tried to heal him, but Peter had protected his wound with all his might until he ended up denying the One he had promised to follow to prison and death. Praise God, he chose to face his splinters and yield them to God.

Years later Peter wrote, "Forasmuch then as Christ hath suffered for us in the flesh, arm yourselves likewise with the same mind: for he that has suffered in the flesh has ceased from sin; that he no longer should live the rest of his time in the flesh to the lusts of men, but to the will of God."[6]

Peter learned to see suffering as an opportunity for growth, a chance to remove the splinters and lay down the defensive shield. He realized that suffering is one of the means God uses to restore His image in us. He saw that the attitude of embracing suffering protects us

---

3. See Matthew 16:21, 22.
4. Verse 23, NKJV.
5. Verses 24, 25, NIV.
6. 1 Peter 4:1, 2.

from becoming false martyrs and puts us on the path to triumph. Peter picked up his cross and followed Christ, who "learned obedience by the things which he suffered."[7]

Get it out!

Albert felt like Peter at first—he'd rather avoid suffering. He was tempted to deny or shield his splinter, to just put up with it, or to lash out at those who were bumping it. But he made a different choice. He recognized that the storm without was triggering a storm within because of the embedded splinter in his life. He sensed that the only way to find peace in the midst of the storm would be to remove the offending splinter.

But he had no idea how to do it. That's when he realized, for the first time in his life, that he really needed God. He had loved God and served God all of his life. But now, he *needed* God! He not only embraced the suffering—he embraced God in the suffering. As Jacob wrestled with the angel through the night, Albert grasped God pleading, " 'I will not let thee go, except thou bless me.' "[8]

And God did not fail him! He showed Albert what the splinter was and where it had come from. And then He gave Albert a simple program for removing it.

"Albert," He instructed, *"every time you sense these thoughts and feelings of rejection coming into your mind, I want you to recognize that they are not from Me and that you don't have to accept them. Simply give them to Me, and I will give you other thoughts to replace them. The painful emotions won't be gone immediately, but they will subside in time.*

"This is a process you will have to repeat over and over again, because the splinter has been there for a long time. Eventually, though, it will be all gone, and people will be able to bump you there, and, though the bump may be painful, it won't elicit the response of rejection you now experience."

This prescription sounds simple, but for Albert, it was like facing the Red Sea. He felt walled in on both sides by his circumstances while his frenemies were pursuing him from behind and the impassable sea of his

---

7. Hebrews 5:8, NKJV.
8. Genesis 32:26.

pain lay before him. God asked him to step into the sea. He did, and God opened the way before him.

Albert was shopping at the local hardware store one day when he ran into Sam. Instantly the thought came to him, *You have displeased Sam. So he doesn't accept you. You're rejected, a misfit! Withdraw into quiet despair. You're no good.*

"Lord," Albert cried out silently, "there are those feelings of rejection. What would You have me replace them with?"

"Albert, I loved you while you were still at odds with Me.[9] *I have loved you with an everlasting love.*[10] *You are accepted in My beloved Son, Jesus.*[11] *I have called you and not rejected you.*[12] *Don't take in the rejection—live above it by taking in My love."*

Albert cooperated. He chose to dwell on God's unconditional love for him instead of the apparent rejection of his friend. As he did so, God transformed his feelings, and Albert found peace instead of pain. Albert's prayer and God's response to his mind happened in a matter of seconds. But Albert was still facing Sam.

"Lord, what would You have me do with Sam?"

"Instead of withdrawing timidly, smile at him and say, 'Hello.'"

Albert smiled a friendly greeting, but Sam turned around and walked the other way.

"Lord, it didn't work. He still treated me like an enemy."

"That's OK. That's his choice. But you don't have to live under his choice. You can live in the reality that you are accepted and beloved in Me, and that will lift you above the rejection of your frenemies."

As Albert moved forward, facing situation after situation that triggered his feelings of rejection, he applied God's prescription, and he did find healing. He found peace in the midst of his storm. His frenemies continued to jostle him and bump him, but he no longer absorbed the rejection. Unlike Lena and Toby, Albert found freedom from bondage.

He didn't regret the suffering he experienced in allowing God to remove the splinter from his life. The freedom of having it gone was like

---

9. See Romans 5:6–8.
10. See Jeremiah 31:3.
11. See Ephesians 1:6.
12. See Isaiah 43:1.

nothing he had experienced before. He could sing the song of Moses and the song of the Lamb—the song of deliverance—because he had tasted for himself God's power to redeem him in areas where he was powerless.

"Icicle mouth"

"Hey, Beaver!" "Buck Teeth!" "Bucky Beaver!" For me, it started in second grade.

My sister, Louise, and I had been playing horsey in our living room. She was the bucking bronco, and I was the cowboy. All went well until the bronco bucked a little too hard, and the cowboy sailed into the coffee table mouth-first. Momentarily stunned, I began wailing as blood spurted out of my mouth. My mother rushed into the room and quickly checked my injury. My two front teeth had been knocked out. Sticking them back in place, she hurriedly drove me to the orthodontist.

Dr. Kloehn examined my mouth carefully. Unfortunately, these had been my new permanent teeth. Dr. Kloehn felt that the best thing to do was to try to save them. So he fashioned a mold around them, hoping they'd reset themselves.

The mold made my upper lip protrude over my lower lip and looked kind of funny. It also caused me to speak with a lisp. Aside from the obvious discomfort, I wondered if anyone at school would notice. Notice? Did they ever!

Now I was "different" from the other second-graders. When you're different, you are going to be wounded. My peer group hurled names at me like "icicle mouth," "lispy," and "beaver." Those who didn't join in the name-calling either laughed or watched silently. I felt alone, rejected—and through those emotions, a lie was injected into my subconscious just like a splinter is jabbed deep into the flesh. *You're not good enough unless you're like everyone else. You don't measure up. You don't belong. You're a misfit.*

As a child of eight, I was not equipped to recognize those emotion-driven lies for what they were. I believed them. I took them in. They became part of my reality—the reality of rejection. And it hurt—just like a splinter does!

I was already a shy boy, but now I withdrew even further, trying to avoid more splinters. I crawled into a shell—a self-protective shield of introversion that I thought would protect me. The problem was that the splinter was already there. I had already internalized the messages of those taunts, and they wounded me afresh as my mind rehearsed them from within my shell.

When my turn came in reading class, I'd stand with eyes down, trembling, breathing hard. My voice would be barely audible as I'd read my part. I would return to my seat—cringing at the snickers and snide remarks that my classmates sent my way. I was entering the brotherhood of the walking wounded. Can you identify with me?

Others in my class suffered as I did. Even now, I can readily remember the names, the taunts the other kids gave to the fattest boy, the homeliest girl, the clumsiest kid, the class dunce, and the shy little girl they called "four eyes." Wounded in heart and mind only because they were different—because they didn't match the "norm." How about you? Have you been there? Are you there right now?

That seemed to be my story all the way through grade school, high school, and college—and into my careers. It's not that I tried to be different. For some reason, I just was.

In grade school, I withdrew. Because I was of only average intelligence, wasn't overly talented in competitive sports, and didn't possess an outgoing personality, I simply remained aloof. That would become my protective shield.

High school challenged me. I discovered that I had abilities in track. Because of my speed and agility, I did well as a halfback on the football team. This put me with the "in crowd." There was only one problem. The "in crowd" did things I didn't feel were "in." All the jocks were trying out their girlfriends the way you try on a pair of shoes before you buy them or test-drive a car before you purchase it. "Come on, Jim," they prodded. "Get with it!"

But I wanted a girl just like the girl who married dear old Dad—pure, virtuous, and untarnished. I treasured Sally's heart more than the thrill of exploiting her just so I could "fit in." They called me square, prudish, old-fashioned. My choice was either to surrender my principles or not to fit in. I chose not to fit in. (By the way, I have no regrets!)

Then college days arrived. Drinking parties, X-rated movies, "girlie" shows—the "in crowd." Sloppy dress, goofy talk, Earth Day, the Vietnam War. It seemed I was always the odd one out. I tried some of this "in" stuff, but it wasn't me. I didn't know then about the voice of one's conscience, and neither had I read the Scriptures. But I just couldn't get into what most of the others were doing. I dressed differently, talked differently, and had different goals and standards from my peers.

I didn't understand. I always thought that there was something weird about me. It's not that I never ventured on some of this ground. It's that when I did, I couldn't live that way. I was becoming an "albino squirrel."

The albino squirrel syndrome

Phantom was the most handsome squirrel I've ever laid eyes on. His snow-white fur and pink eyes, ears, and nose set him apart from the other squirrels in the backyard of our Shiocton, Wisconsin, home. We loved seeing him and always welcomed him to our feeder. But not so, his siblings. They would chase him, nip at him, bite him, and drive him deep into the woods, where he lived in fear of the other squirrels. One day I followed the ruckus and discovered his hideout—an old solitary oak tree.

Even as an adult, I identified with Phantom. He was different from the other squirrels, and he was rejected. He coped with rejection in the same way I had—he withdrew and hid. My heart was knit with his heart. I began to bring him nuts and sunflower seeds. Gradually, he began to trust me and let me get close. Over time, we became friends. I was probably the only friend Phantom ever had. Then our family moved to the wilderness of Montana. I felt like I was abandoning him. I wanted to take Phantom with us. It may sound corny, but my heart ached for that little fellow. He was rejected not only by his peers but also by his family.

All my life, it seemed that I was abandoned for being an "albino squirrel." My family and friends abandoned me when I changed from being Catholic to being a fundamentalist, Bible-believing Protestant. My family and friends saw me as a sheep that had put on wolves' clothing. My parents removed my name from their will. My siblings would have little or nothing to do with me. My old partying buddies didn't call anymore. Those splinters went *deep*. Deeper than you might think. Why? Because they echoed the powerful lie I had embraced in childhood, high school, and college: *You are the albino squirrel. When you are different from everyone else, you don't fit in. You're a misfit. Your acceptance and belonging is conditional upon being like everyone else.* And this new rejection I experienced as an adult reinforced what I had learned as a child.

"Mr. Lonely"

Because I subconsciously believed that lie, I became "Mr. Lonely." Oh, I laughed on the outside, but I was bleeding on the inside. Sure, I met new friends. Sure, I developed a new church family. But I was still part of the walking wounded. I was still a "victim." Are you? I still faced rejection the same way I had as a child—I withdrew. Do you?

For years, I also denied that the splinter existed. I unwittingly built my existence around protecting it from being bumped. And when someone bumped it, my natural response was to lash out at him or her. God tempered my irritation, but He wanted to do more for me than just quiet my response when the splinter was bumped.

Facing my firing squad brought me face to face with my splinter. The turmoil I experienced as described earlier in this book was not just about facing that firing squad—it was also about facing my splinter.

The urge to run and hide in denial was strong. The desire to just capitulate and live with the splinter tugged at me. The impulse to lash out at those who kept jabbing the splinter was powerful. But my God kept saying, *"Face it, Jim. Face it with Me."*

I went down into despair—heartrending despair. I felt hopeless. The rejection throbbed so painfully. I felt like Moses at the Red Sea; it seemed the water would swallow me up. I looked for a way back or up or out—and there was none. My God encouraged me, *"Go forward, Jim. Step into the sea."*

I couldn't bring myself to do it. It was going to engulf me. I was going to drown. I barely left my bedroom. At night, I couldn't sleep. During the day, I would find myself weeping on my bed at times. "How, Lord, how? Isn't there another way?" I pleaded. "Can't You remove this splinter from me without my going through this?"

My family members came up to my bedroom to comfort me, to console me, to encourage me to face the trial with God. My faithful wife, Sally, urged me to identify the lies in the accusations being hurled at me by my frenemies, but I couldn't do it. I was no longer just the walking wounded. I was down—disabled—ready to die.

Would I ever find peace? Would I ever be able to sing the song of Moses and the song of the Lamb?

CHAPTER 6

THE WALKING WOUNDED

Questions to Consider for Personal Inventory or Group Discussions

1. Have you wounded others?
2. Is the Holy Spirit prompting you to go to those you have wounded and make things right?
3. Are you one of the walking wounded?
4. Have you experienced the splinter of rejection?
5. Which of the five options for dealing with splinters given in this chapter do you choose to use?
6. Is there some of "Lena" or "Toby" in you?
7. Are your splinters self-imposed?
8. Are you on the path of triumph or the path of false martyrdom?
9. Can you embrace your suffering or splinter "with Christ"?

Peace Amidst the Storm

Thou wilt keep him in perfect peace, whose mind is stayed on thee.
—Isaiah 26:3

Have you ever felt as if you were in a dark, deep pit with no way of escape, no hope of sunlight, and no one to rescue you? Do you know what it means to feel locked in a tomb you can't see beyond—and to sense that your future holds nothing more than this?

When my frenemy fire hit, it hit hard. It wasn't outsiders who were trying to undo me. It was my friends, my spiritual soul mates, my kindred spirits. I can't begin to describe the confusion of painful emotions that surged through my being—the self-doubt, the questioning, the despair. The storm without kindled a raging firestorm within. Would I survive?

At the same time this turmoil was going on in my life, Larry asked to talk with me—privately and in person. Larry had been one of my closest friends. I had trusted him, respected him, and valued his perspective in spiritual matters. Yet over the months, our relationship had deteriorated. Reports had circulated back to me of half-truths and innuendos coming from Larry. To my face, he had become distant, critical, and demanding. He insisted that I view things as he did. He claimed I was stubborn, proud, and disconnected from God. Was he right?

His request to meet with me carried with it the overtones of another unsolvable confrontation. In the context of everything else that was going on, I just didn't think I could face it. The entire situation rose up before me like a tsunami poised to drown me.

I lay on my bed, my mind swirling with confusion. The voices of my frenemies shouted loudly, *"You're wrong, Jim. You are misrepresenting God, Jim. If you don't conform to our views, Jim, you are going to be ruined. If you won't operate under our agenda, consider yourself finished. There is no hope for you. You are done. Give up and capitulate!"*

The splinter of my past rejection screamed at me, *You never fit in, Jim. You're always the odd man out, the "albino squirrel." There's something wrong with you. Why do you always have to be different? Comply and fit in. Meet their standards. Gain their acceptance. Do whatever it takes to pacify them so they will like you!*

Other splinters shrieked out their demands too. There was the splinter of my reputation. I had been raised to guard the family name with my life. *Whatever you do, Jim, protect your reputation. Do not allow it to be dragged through the mire. Do not permit anything to tarnish it. Do whatever it takes to preserve it.*

The splinter of fear sent its chilling message straight to my core. *If you don't bend, Jim, you will lose your ministry and your livelihood. You will have no means of supporting your family. That will mean you are a failure as a man—a washout, a loser!*

I had always taken very seriously my responsibility to provide for my family. I could not conceive of life apart from being able to fulfill this part of my duty to them. God had called me out of the real-estate business into full-time ministry. One of my sons now covered the territory in the north valley that I had once marketed. I couldn't go back into real estate and compete against my son. That wasn't an option. Yet I could see nowhere else to go.

The fourth splinter shouted, *You will lose your comfortable life, Jim. You will lose all your friends. No one will stand by you. They will all desert you. You won't be able to afford to support your family. You'll lose your home, all your possessions—everything that makes life comfortable. You can't be happy if you're not comfortable.*

Taken away

I felt as if I were back in kindergarten. I had spent my first month of kindergarten hiding under my teacher's desk. I was so shy, so introverted, and so scared that I wouldn't come out except for recess and to go home.

That's how I felt now. *I'm just a reject, and I want to hide and protect myself. I can't face it. I can't fix it. I can't meet it. It will kill me.*

I grew up never fitting in. Yet I had wanted desperately to be "somebody." I had wanted to be important. I had wanted to be influential. I had wanted to make a lot of money because that would make me "somebody." I had wanted friends. I had wanted people to like me. I had wanted to be popular.

When I graduated from college and married the best woman in the world, I began to achieve my dreams. In sales, my insurance agency was rated in the top 10 percent with the fifth-largest mutual insurance company in the nation. I brought home a six-figure income. I made friends and found myself popular. I became an elder in the church and brought a number of other people into the church. People looked up to me. I was becoming "somebody."

Then God called me to walk away from all this to search for a genuine walk with Him. I wrestled and struggled and finally made the decision to leave it all behind and move to a little log cabin in the north woods of Montana. That step of faith proved to be solid, and I found myself enjoying a growing spiritual walk, a revitalized marriage, and a connected family—all supported by a prosperous real-estate business. Life was comfortable again.

And that's when God again called me to walk away from my prosperous business and enter full-time ministry. He asked me to depend wholly on Him for my livelihood. I had no idea where the calls for ministry would come from or how I would put food on my family's table, but God asked me to step forward in faith. Once again, I wrestled and struggled and finally came to the decision to take God at His Word and move forward.

And He had blessed. From a small beginning, the ministry had grown remarkably. Lives were being changed. Marriages were being restored. Families were being reconnected. It was good. It was rewarding.

Now, it seemed that God was not *asking me to walk away.* Rather, it seemed that He was *taking it all away*—or allowing it to be taken. And He didn't give me a picture of anything that lay ahead. What before had always been a step of faith, now appeared to be a step into oblivion with nothing in sight to catch me.

"Where are You, God?" I demanded. "Why are You so silent? Why can't You show me the next step? Why can't You tell me the next line in this script?"

I was floundering, sinking, drowning. The voices in my head got louder and louder, mixing together into one dissonant cacophony. The more I focused on them, the louder they got. They presented to me the worst possible scenario—and I believed them.

I mentally reviewed the situation again and again, trying in vain to fix it, to solve it, to turn it around. I argued with these dissonant thoughts, trying to reason them through. When you continue to focus on a problem, there soon appears to be no hope, no future, and no one who can turn it around or fix it. You feel doomed, deserted, and in need of divine help. That's where I was.

"God, where are You when I need You? I can't sense You or hear You. Have You abandoned me too?"

Where is He?

It seemed that God was silent. In hindsight, I recognize that He was prompting me to stop my endless rehearsing and begin to evaluate—evaluate each of the voices.

Like Elijah in the cave on Mount Horeb, I wanted to know where God's voice was. For Elijah, it was not in the wind, not in the earthquake, not in the fire. It was a still, small Voice independent of the stormy elements.[1] I began evaluating. Was God in my storm? Was He in the stormy voices from without—my frenemies? Were they echoing the voice of God? How could I know?

"By their fruits ye shall know them."[2]

But what kind of fruit should I look for? Their motive and approach would be big clues. "Where the Spirit of the Lord is, there is liberty."[3] Were they granting me the same liberty that God grants me, or were they bearing the mark of Cain? Were they like a salesman who pressures me to make a decision *now,* or were they giving me the same freedom that God gives when He says, "Come now, and let us reason together"?[4]

---

1. See 1 Kings 19:11, 12.
2. Matthew 7:20.
3. 2 Corinthians 3:17.
4. Isaiah 1:18.

I had to honestly admit that they gave more evidence of the mark of Cain than of the Spirit of the Lord.

Were they giving evidence of having a predetermined heart or a listening heart? I tried to dispassionately evaluate their procedures and the way they were conducting affairs between us. As best I could evaluate, they were displaying a predetermined heart. For them, there was no solution other than for me to yield my conscience to their dictates.

Did their charges line up with Scripture? Were their accusations validated by the Word of God? "To the law and to the testimony: if they speak not according to this word, it is because there is no light in them."[5] While they quoted the Scriptures, their accusations were based on misconstruing them—not a plain "Thus saith the Lord."

The voice of God was not there.

Was He in the stormy voices arising from within me—my splinters? Were they the voice of God?

I had to recognize that every one of those voices centered on me, myself—*my* acceptance, *my* reputation, *my* livelihood, *my* comfort. The choices they suggested did not line up with the principles of God's Word or the life exemplified by Christ. They were all about self-preservation, looking out for number one. They told me that other people would determine my destiny. I didn't like that. I wanted control. I wanted to manage my own choices.

I could see that the voice of God was not there either—His voice was not in the storm without or the storm within. "Where are You, God? I can't hear You."

Opening my Bible, I turned to Hebrews 13:5: " 'I will never leave you nor forsake you' " (NKJV). There was the still, small Voice—exceedingly quiet in contrast with the clamor in my own head. Which voice was true? Which was reliable? Which would I act on? The intimidating voice of my frenemies? The self-protective voice of my splinters? Or the naked promise of God?

Two realities

I had a choice to make. The storm from without clamored, *They've got you down, Jim. Humanly speaking, there's no way out. You are done.*

---

5. Isaiah 8:20.

Capitulate! Capitulate! Capitulate! The storm from within shrieked in my ears, *You have no assurance of the outcome. You don't know how long it will last or how difficult it will be. Fight or flee!*

The still, small Voice simply inquired, *"Will you trust Me?"*

I broke out in a cold sweat as I contemplated my options. Fear wrestled with trust. *God was with Daniel when he faced the den of lions and with the three Hebrews in the fiery furnace. They didn't know if God would preserve them, but He did. I, too, can trust God. But Daniel and his three friends were more worthy than I am. They weren't so full of faults and weaknesses as I am. God might not be with me the way He was with them.*

I wrestled and wrestled. For nearly two days I wrestled. Like Jacob beside the Brook Jabbok,[6] I wrestled—not fully discerning what I was wrestling with. Finally, I realized that God was calling for total surrender to Him. He was asking for absolute trust that He is in ultimate control of my life and my future. God—not circumstances, not frenemies, not politics, not even me—was to have the final say in all things. God was asking me to lay down everything—to relinquish all I had and all I knew to Him.

Laying it down

One man invited another to join him on a wilderness canoe trip. Arriving at their launching site, they each loaded their packs on their backs and carried the canoe down to the lake. The owner of the canoe took off his pack, laid it in the bottom of the canoe, and climbed in. Sitting down in the rear of the canoe, he swung the bow around so his friend could step in.

Upon stepping into the canoe, his friend began to paddle with his pack on. Puzzled, the first man asked, "Why don't you lay your pack in the bottom of the canoe?"

"Oh," his friend replied, "it's so generous of you to invite me on this canoe trip. It seems like a lot for me to expect the canoe to carry *me*. I can't expect it to carry my pack as well!"

The second canoeist in the parable illustrates me! Does he illustrate you? I was willing to give myself to God, but I was struggling with the

---

6. See Genesis 32:22–30.

idea that I needed to lay everything down and depend only on Him! Like a three-year-old being asked to surrender his favorite "blankie" to a loving father, I wrestled and agonized. Would I do it? Would I trust Him?

My "blankie" was my reputation, my future, my livelihood, my purpose for living, and my comfort. Would I give it to God and rest my entire weight, my entire load, my future, my hurt, my fears—everything—upon Him? Would I cast all my care upon Him who cares for me?[7]

I made the decision to act on God's quiet voice—the one confirmed in Scripture. I chose to abandon myself to His grace.

Broken at last, I bowed my head,
Forgetting all myself, and said,
"Whatever comes, His will be done,"
And in that moment peace was won.
—Henry Van Dyke

El Shaddai

Instead of finding annihilation, I found peace. Instead of destruction, I felt like living again. Instead of oblivion, I found hope! It didn't matter anymore. All that mattered was that God would have the final say!

He's El Shaddai, the all-sufficient One! He is sufficient for me! He is sufficient for you! He's not just the God of the past. He's the God of the present, and the future—and He always has the last word!

I eagerly opened the Psalms—written so many years ago by someone who faced a more intimidating annihilation than I had faced. I could identify with his wrestlings and his resting in God. Psalm 62:5 was like a lifesaver for a man just getting his head above the water. "My soul, wait thou only upon God; for my expectation is from him."

It was God that I needed. He was always there; He would never leave me, never forsake me; and there would never be anything too difficult for Him to fix. I dwelt upon His promise until I believed it more than I believed all the threatenings of my dark pit. Faith became a greater

---

7. See 1 Peter 5:7.

reality than my circumstances—faith in a God that would lead me through my dark nights.

Again and again I read, recited, and focused on His promises. Guess what? I was freed. Freed from my fears. Freed from sorrow and despair. The clamoring storm without couldn't touch me without His permission. The raging storm within was gone! I had found El Shaddai—the God of my flesh, the God for whom nothing is too hard. I had thrown myself utterly into His hands and trusted Him as I had never before done. I found, by experience, that He doesn't desert us or sell us out. He doesn't smear our name, play politics, or block our future. He's always there no matter what. His is not a conditional love—a love with a big *if*. No! His love is without any *ifs*. His love is long-suffering; it endures forever.

Sure, I had made mistakes. If we're honest, we'll admit that we all do. That's why I need a Savior—One who comes to my side, lifts me up, and restores me into His image.

"O God, thank You for this dark moment in my life. Thank You for the hurt, the sorrow, and the suffering. It has helped me to find You in a deeper way. Lord, by Your grace, through faith, I choose to put away my fears, my sorrow, and my despair; I choose to depend utterly upon you, El Shaddai—the All-Sufficient One!"

"And thank you, frenemies, for helping me to gain a stronger hold on the Prince of my peace. Thank you for helping me find rest in the midst of my anxiety. Thank you for teaching me how to let go and let God."

God can, and does, use the evil of this world to bring about good. Along with Horatio Spafford, I could truly say, "It is well with my soul."

Live above the storm

I went to my meeting with Larry—not filled with dread and despair, but resting in El Shaddai. We met near the river halfway between my house and town. When I got out of my car, a smile wreathed my face.

"Larry," I shouted, "I'm free! I'm free! I'm set free!"

I hugged him and swung him around and around. I was ecstatic. It didn't matter anymore what happened to me as long as God was in charge.

He looked at me as if I had lost my mind. Then he started in. For an hour he drilled into me his prophecies of doom and his advice to capitulate. Then, without giving me an opportunity to ask any questions, clarify any misinformation, or to present my convictions, he left.

But I was free! I had peace in the midst of my storm. I began to see that this experience was good medicine. Even though God doesn't create such frenemy fire, He calls us out of these black holes—waiting and desiring to lift us up. He did that with David as he was hunted like a dog by King Saul, and with Joseph as his brothers sold him as a slave. Likewise, God uses these devastating experiences to free us from our splinters and set us at liberty.

The fixing to be done wasn't so much with these things as it was with me. When I laid it all down in the midst of my storm—by choosing to believe that God is bigger than my circumstances; by choosing to say no to the lying thoughts and yes to God's promises; by choosing not to retaliate or seek vengeance; by accepting that suffering is a positive part of dross burning—peace, wonderful peace, came in, and I was free! Free to let God fight for me! Free to not retaliate! Free to get on with living! Free to look up and live! Set free in the midst of the storm!

It's available to all—rich or poor; educated or illiterate; talented or handicapped. God offers His peace and rest unconditionally to all of His children—regardless of circumstance. We have but to enter into it, hold on to it, and never let it go.

I thought that after that experience I would always have peace. I thought I would never have to go through that again. But I was mistaken. I had to face that battle again and again until I learned to hold on. I began to notice the pattern. First would come the confusion triggered by some fresh outbreak of frenemy fire. Then I would need to evaluate what spirit was behind the new accusation or approach and discern what God was saying to me through it. Then I must choose which reality and under whose influence I would live.

Look up!

I was at one of our camp meetings—scheduled to speak in just one hour—when a phone call came through for me. It was the pastor of a large church where we had been invited to hold a seminar.

"Jim, I hate to break this news to you right now, but I thought you had a right to know what is going on."

"Yes, Pastor, what is it?"

"Fred and Alice Jones have requested a special hearing with the board of elders at this church. They are adamant that you should not be allowed in the pulpit, and they want to share their reasons why."

Fred and Alice! Why, they had attended many of our meetings! They had been in our home, and we had been in theirs. Our children were about the same ages, and we had enjoyed some special spiritual times together. They had never come to me to share their honest concerns. Apparently, however, they had threatened to do everything they could to shut us down.

"Did they share their reasons with you?" I asked.

"Yes, they did, Jim." And the pastor proceeded to list some of the same false objections that had been raised by my firing squad.

"What are your thoughts, Pastor?"

"We'll give them a chance to make their presentation to the elders, but my impression is that they have a personal problem with you. We'll see what the elders think."

My emotions rapidly slid back into that pit of rejection. The voice of my frenemies started shouting inside my head again. *"See, Jim. We will have the last word. We will control your future. You can't escape us!"*

My splinters started throbbing and screaming out, *You're a reject, Jim. You're losing your reputation, your livelihood, your comfort. You'd better do something to protect yourself.*

The still, small Voice was there as well, but it seemed so quiet in comparison. And I was supposed to be entering the pulpit to preach about the God who will never leave us or forsake us!

I took a seat on one side of the auditorium as the service got underway. I wrestled in my mind. My emotions were stirred up. My thoughts were disquieted. I was endeavoring to grasp my El Shaddai, but I was floundering.

"God, for Your sake and the sake of Your people, please help me!"

Just then, I felt a gentle tap on my shoulder. "Lord, I can't talk to anyone right now. I've got to go up front in a few moments, and I need to connect with You. What am I going to do with this person who is interrupting me right now?"

"Just listen, Jim."

I turned to see Joanne kneeling in the aisle beside me. "Jim, I know you're going up to speak in a few moments, but I felt impressed to share something with you. I've recently learned something about the turmoil you are facing right now, and I've been praying for you. This morning I was out walking and praying, and you and Sally were especially on my mind. As I lifted you up before God, a picture came to my mind of a dark, ugly tornado. It was swirling and pulling up all kinds of dirt and debris—and you were in the middle of it. At first I thought you were going to be swept away by it. But then I recognized that you were in the eye of the storm where it was peaceful and quiet.

"As I prayed for you, I saw that if you step out ahead of the Lord or lag behind, you'll be sucked into the fierce storm. Also, if you veer to the left or right you will be swept into the raging wind. But as long as you stand in the eye of the tornado and keep looking up, cooperating with Jesus, you are safe."

Look up! That's not what the devil wants! No, he wants us to focus on the storm! To get into it. To duke it out. They hit you; you hit them. Just the way the presidential candidates do it. Smear their name. Bring on the false accusations.

The swirling tornado demands our attention. It insists we step into it. Why? Because there is no hope in the problem! It's nothing more than a death march. By concentrating our attention on the storm, we step into it. We take in that which is not necessary. We take upon ourselves the false accusations and insidious implications—what they think and what they demand—and these become new splinters. We begin to fear their plottings and reprisals. We submit to despair.

The other ditch

Even more insidious, but no less dangerous, is the opposite error. We see their actions for what they are. As we dwell on them, their "evil" begins to grow in contrast with our "righteousness." When we start to feel superior to someone else, we lose our hold on God, who is our only sufficiency.

That's dangerous! We need to hold on to the reality that "all have sinned"—including us! We *all* need grace. We must be willing to see *our* shortcomings and blind spots. We must admit *our* mistakes—even if it seems like our part of the problem is only 5 percent in comparison with their 95 percent. We need to admit our downside and make right all that is in our power to change. This is difficult because often our best efforts are inadequate to resolve the problem. We still are the target of frenemy fire. It still throws at us all kinds of curves, detours, half-truths, and innuendos. When a person is born with a high sense of justice, as I was, only a deeper and deeper humility will keep us out of either the ditch of despair on the one hand or the ditch of self-righteous superiority on the other.

That morning as I was preparing to speak to the people, the devil wanted me to lose my purpose, focus, and courage. He wanted me to compromise my principles and capitulate my conscience. So he endeavored to cloud the issues and place a smoke screen in my path. God, on the other hand, wanted me to climb through the cloud and press through the smoke screen. He wanted me to learn not to stop for the barking dogs.

Don't stop for the barking dogs!

A friend of mine used to work the railway lines. He told me how stray dogs used to hang around the station and sleep under the railway cars that were parked to the side of the station. The dogs never barked at the parked cars. But if a moving train came through, they'd all jump up, bark ferociously, and chase the train as if they were going to take it down. The only way to stop them was to either bring the train to a halt or outrun them.

My friend advised, "Jim, don't stop for the barking dogs!"

I was so tempted to lose my focus, to get distracted from God, to preach to the people while my mind was dealing with my frenemies. I wanted to stop and give the barking dogs a piece of my mind.

But God was calling. *"Jim, look up. Look up to Me! Don't focus on the dirt or the debris. Don't worry about the strong wind that wants to suck you into its control. Don't stop for the barking dogs. Look to Me. Follow Me. I still have the final word for you!"*

To look up is to admit that I can't fix my problem or resolve it. It is realizing that it amounts to no saving good to try to change circumstance or convince others that I am right. It is surrendering my need to be understood, vindicated, and have the problem resolved. It means I'm releasing control to God. That's scary, because I'm putting my future into the hands of One I can't see, hear, or personally talk with. Sure He's there—but not in the tangible way we'd like. To look up means that we come to a point where we trust that God will fight for us while we hold our peace.[8] Why? Because God is the Architect of our way out.

God, the Architect

God's ways are not our ways. He works behind the scenes while we move on with what He wants us to deal with—usually our thought life, our emotions, and the work He has called us to do.

Does God intervene? Of course He does, but He—not us—writes the script. Neither David, Joseph, Wycliffe, nor Luther could perceive how God was going to intervene in his behalf. They could not predict His timing or His methods. No, He's the God of the universe. We must leave the pen in the Architect's hand—not take it in our own.

So often I'm tempted to say, "Lord, give me the pen." You see, I'd write a different script for myself. I'd write in a bit more sunshine and silver slippers. Perhaps a South Pacific island with a hammock and some lemonade. I'd bring down justice on my frenemies, perhaps some immediate vengeance. *Ouch!* Is that how Christ has dealt with me through the years? Doesn't Romans 2:4 state "that the *goodness* of God leads you to repentance" (NKJV; emphasis added)? Why is it that we want that prescription to apply to us and not to them?

My faith was tested and tried in the crucible of adversity. God said, *"Trust Me."*

"But, Lord, these are professed Christians—not worldlings."

"It doesn't matter, Jim. You need to let go of your circumstances and trust Me. Don't stop for the barking dogs. They will always be there. Forgive and move on. Let Me deal with your frenemies."

---

8. See Exodus 14:14.

The journey of forgiveness

"Forgive them, Lord?" I know I'm supposed to forgive them, but my emotions are just not there. My sense of justice far outweighs my sense of mercy. "How could they do this to me? Who do they think they are? Just give me a chance to get even with them."

"*Jim.*"

"Yes, Lord."

"*How many years did you mistreat Me? Have you forgotten that you are a sinner in need of grace too?*"

For me, forgiveness has been a journey—not a moment. I would make a principled decision to forgive—to release the cancer of bitterness that wanted to take root in my heart. And I would find peace. The clamoring emotions would be subdued, and I could pray for my frenemies. Then would come some fresh report of frenemy fire, or I would run into one of my frenemies at the airport, and all the old emotions would instantly be alive—and I would have to go through the same process again.

Some have said that forgiving is forgetting. I don't believe that is true. Forgetting is *not* the same as forgiving. Forgetting is simply amnesia. Forgiving is a process of removing the pain from a memory. It is relinquishing to God our desire to retaliate. It is internalizing the reality of how great is our debt to God in comparison with the debt our brother owes us. Forgiveness can be done whether or not the party who wronged us recognizes their wrong and makes restitution.

Forgiveness is not the same as reconciliation. For reconciliation to take place, there must be an establishment of trust on both sides. When trust has been severely violated—such as in the case of Joseph and his brothers or with Jesus and Peter—trustworthiness must be proved and tested in order for the relationship to be restored.

"OK, Lord. I'll forgive them on principle and trust You to subdue my clamoring emotions. But, Lord, You're not telling me how You're going to work out this situation. You're not revealing to me Your counterplan. You're not assuring me that the lions won't take me out. If You're the Architect, why can't I see the final draft? Why can't I see the whole set of blueprints? Why, Lord, why?"

"*Jim, embrace Me fully, completely, and utterly. Trust in Me. Then, in confidence, go about the work I've called you to. Let Me handle all that goes on behind the scenes. Move on, Jim. This is a trial of your faith. This will deepen your trust in Me. Put away your anxious spirit and rest in Me until you find that peace that passes all understanding."*

I heard the call, and I made my choice. "OK, Lord. I relinquish control to You."

My faith took hold of the unseen reality, and as I took the pulpit that day, I could preach with heartfelt assurance about my El Shaddai—my All-Sufficient One! He was there. In my necessity, He came through. Surrendering to Him, depending on Him, believing in Him brought me peace in the midst of my storm once again. What had been a long drawn out battle before was now resolved in less than an hour.

Resting in the crucible

I faced that same battle again and again. God in His great wisdom allows us to be tested and tried in the areas that worry us most. That which we fear most is the area we will be tried in the most. Why? Because an all-loving God doesn't want externals to control us!

He wants us to be anxious for nothing. He wants us to rest always in Him, fearing lest we come short of His peace. This is to be the present experience of every believer—fully surrendered and totally resting in his Savior in the here and now.

Is there anything in your life that occupies your thoughts all the time? Some idol, some fear, worry, or hurt? If there is, then God will allow you to be tested and tried over and over again until you lay it all down. Lay down those plaguing thoughts, those uncontrollable emotions, all those anxieties—and rest in your God. He is your Helper. He will never leave you nor forsake you. You don't need to fear what man can do to you.[9] El Shaddai is present with you and will carry you through one day, one moment, at a time. The unseen God is there for you!

So much of our unrest is in our thoughts and emotions. Go ahead, give them to God. Give them again and again until they are laid down. This is not a one-time achievement. No, it's a journey of discovery—discovering that personal peace comes from total abandonment to God. It means learning to be very *active* in trusting that God is ultimately in charge while being very *passive* in responding to the clamoring

9. See Hebrews 13:5, 6.

emotions of fear, despair, anxiety, rejection, hurt, concern for my reputation, and inconvenience.

You may be thinking, *Do you mean that it amounts to no saving good to rehearse my thoughts again and again? Do you mean I must exchange my thoughts and wounded spirit for His love and His promises? Are you saying that this is a mind battle? That I must let the mind of Christ become my mind?[10] That I must choose to think on that which is true, honest, just, pure, lovely, virtuous, and of a good report?[11]*

Precisely!

"But that's hard," you say.

Oh, it gets easier. The formula is simple—total surrender to God. To be totally abandoned to God is to be totally at peace. It's just that simple. But it is oh so hard at first.

Hard because we want to be in charge. We want to be the architect over our Architect. We want to write the script. We want assurances that the outcome will be as we would write it. That's just our problem. We believe in God, but we don't trust in God. So God has to deliver us for our own sake. He has to free us—not so much from our frenemies, but from ourselves.

Sure, we have rough edges. That's why He allows these trials. He's the Silversmith. He'll allow only the dross to be consumed in the fire. He won't forsake you. He's our Helper, our Architect. Search your conscience, make right any wrongs until your conscience is free.

If your conscience is free, then live free. Stop focusing on the problem. Stop mulling it over a thousand and one times in your head. Quit rehearsing it in your emotions, and quit repeating it to everyone you run into. Rise above it, get beyond it, and live free as as if it never happened or has been fully resolved.

Live in the expectation (faith) that your God is ultimately in control (grace). Be a Daniel. Go to your God in prayer, and when your frenemies consort to throw you into the lions' den, don't fear! God can shut the mouths of the lions. Daniel's conscience was free, so he lived free. That's faith! A real live, present, active, ongoing faith that your God is the Architect in control.

---

10. See Philippians 2:5.
11. See Philippians 4:8.

The great, grand secret of peace in the midst of the storm is learning how to obtain and retain His perpetual presence with us—and then to rest in it continually. Solomon, the wisest man who ever lived, said, "All is vanity, except oneness with God."[12] We are to find that unity with Him at all cost, and when we do, realize that we will become a target.

The devil's target

A pastor's wife approached me at one of our seminars. She just had to share a dream she had dreamed about me.

"Jim, I saw many people shooting arrows at you. You were trying to defend and shield yourself. But you were getting hit and even bleeding. Then you saw Jesus standing off in the distance, and He invited you, 'Come.' You ran to Him and stood behind Him. The arrows kept coming, but He deflected every one. Once in a while you would step out from behind Jesus, and sure enough, you'd get hit again."

If you are seeking God with your whole heart, mind, and soul, you are going to become a target. Why? Because the devil is angry and unreasonable and wants to discourage you. He wants to break your connection with God, remove your Shield, and take you captive into his lair—the pit of despair. He does not want you to break free from his control.

I've seen it happen time and time again. People come to one of our seminars. God gets hold of their thoughts and hearts. They endeavor to simplify their lives, prioritize their marriages, revitalize their families, and cultivate their connection with God. Sure enough, everything seems to go wrong.

The psalmist says, "Many are the afflictions of the righteous."[13] Notice that the text says "many," not "few." Afflictions cause us pain—mentally, emotionally, and spiritually. Satan sees you're determined to find God and to serve Him heart and soul. So he stirs up every conceivable frenemy and circumstance to stop you. He knows he had you once, and he is determined to neutralize your spirit.

How does he do this? Through many ways and means. But his most effective method is to incite professed Christians to crucify other Christians. I call those who engage in this activity "Junior Holy Spirits."

---

12. My paraphrase of the message of Ecclesiastes.
13. Psalm 34:19.

CHAPTER 7
PEACE AMIDST THE STORM

Questions to Consider for Personal Inventory or Group Discussions

1. Can you recognize and name your splinters?
2. Does God ever appear to be silent and far from you?
3. Do those who disagree with you carry with them the Spirit of the Lord or the mark of Cain?
4. Are you like the man in the canoe who just couldn't trust the canoe to carry him *and* his pack as well?
5. Do you have a "blankie" you just can't turn over to God—your reputation, your future, your livelihood, or your comfort?
6. Is faith a greater reality to you than your circumstances?
7. Have you found El Shaddai, the All-Sufficient One?
8. Can you thank your frenemies for helping you to gain a stronger hold on El Shaddai?
9. In the middle of your tornado, amidst the swirling debris and dirt, are you able to stay in the eye of the storm and look up?
10. Do you stop for the barking dogs?
11. Do you want to take the pen out of your Architect's hand?
12. Why is the area we fear the most the area in which we are tested the most?
13. Is it true that personal peace comes from a total abandonment to God?
14. Have you found oneness with God amidst your storm?

Junior Holy Spirits

It is an honor for a man to cease from strife: but every fool will be meddling.—Proverbs 20:3

To me, religious intolerance is one of the greatest evils to touch our lives. It comes in many forms. During the Dark Ages the Bible was suppressed, and the power of the Roman Church was supreme. If you veered from the church's teachings, you could expect to be reeducated—by the dungeon, the rack, or the stake. Today's methods of gaining control over the consciences of others are a bit more subtle but are motivated by the same spirit.

The aftermath of having to face my firing squad was the dissolution of my affiliation with my former associates in ministry. Surely, I thought, ending the affiliation would stop the frenemy fire. Surely we could now both pursue our separate callings in freedom. Instead, the attacks escalated.

Privacy invaded

A couple began tapping our home phone. How do I know? I would complete a telephone conversation with one of my sons and hang up. Seconds later, the phone would ring. The callers refused to identify themselves, but would share detailed knowledge of my private conversation with my son and give me their opinions about what I should or should not do. As you can imagine, this was rather disconcerting. Was my private phone line private or not?

Then they took it a step further. They began to interfere with some of the phone counseling I was doing. Someone would confide his or her troubles to me over the phone and after hanging up, the counselee would receive a call from these anonymous people claiming I had turned the case over to them. They would then proceed to share confidential information that made it obvious that either they had been eavesdropping or I had passed on to them the private information.

Of course, our counselees were bewildered. "Jim, we thought we were sharing with you privately. Why didn't you tell us that you would be passing our case to another counselor?" I understood their bewilderment, and I knew that were I in their shoes, I would be tempted to be offended. I began informing everyone who called us on the phone of the possible eavesdropping going on.

My sons—newly married—started getting late-night calls harassing and intimidating them and their wives. These were not prank calls; they were very serious. The content of the threats gave evidence that these people knew our ministry, our beliefs, and us. It was hard for us to imagine, but we had to conclude that those calling us were the "saints." I call them self-appointed "Junior Holy Spirits," trying to act as the master of our consciences by intimidating us through illegal methods.

We called the police, the sheriff, and the FBI—to no avail. Whoever was behind these distressing occurrences possessed a sophisticated knowledge of the electronic devices they were using and were proficient at covering their tracks. This kind of harassment continued for years.

Ostracized

Soon we started receiving hate letters—yes, hate letters—from professed Christians who felt burdened to straighten us out and condemn us if we didn't see things their way. The words from their poisoned pens stung. We couldn't see an ounce of mercy—only venom. The saying "Sticks and stones will break my bones, but words can never hurt me" might sound true to an onlooker but the recipient learns that harsh words can wound the heart and spirit and can inflict deeper suffering than can the stake and the rack.

One individual drafted a fifty-page document attacking me and my sons, their marriages, and their professions. To this day, I have not read it, but I've heard my wife's and sons' opinions of it. Based heavily on misinformation, speculation, and individual perspective, but couched in the language of love and concern, the document was handed out at a large convocation. I didn't know if the writer was trying to win me back or take me out. It felt to me as if he had stuck a hypodermic needle into me and numbed all my feelings.

Then we started receiving another kind of phone call.

"Hi, Jim, this is Pastor Steve."

My mind quickly sorts out who "Pastor Steve" is. He is the pastor who has invited us to be the main speakers at a large convocation. The advertisements have gone out, people are registered to come, and we have booked our flights.

"Yes, Pastor Steve, what can I do for you?"

There was an uncomfortable pause. "Uh, Jim, I don't quite know how to tell you this, but we are going to have to cancel your invitation to speak at our meeting. I'm awfully sorry and wish the situation were different, but it's just not going to work out."

"Well, Pastor, there has to be more to it than that. Would you mind telling me why this sudden change? This appointment has been in place for some time."

"Um . . . er . . . uh . . . well, I'm not really supposed to get into it with you, Jim, but we received a phone call from someone who knows you well, and it just doesn't seem advisable to have a controversial person like you come to the meeting. I'm sorry, Jim, but that's just the way it is."

This scenario occurred more than once—and the charges were always couched in half-truths and innuendos passed on by someone who *seemed* trustworthy.

Where it all began

Half-truths are sometimes more effective than out-and-out lies. The devil is the master of the half-truth. He used it in heaven, and one-third of the angelic host fell for it. He used half-truths with Eve in the Garden of Eden—in a perfect environment with everything she could possibly desire at her fingertips—and she fell for it.

What did she fall for? The opportunity to become a "Junior Holy Spirit."

The devil, in the form of a serpent, promised her, "In the day ye eat thereof, then your eyes shall be opened, and ye shall be as gods, knowing good and evil."[1]

---

1. Genesis 3:5.

"Eve, don't be content with the sphere God has appointed you. You are capable of a lot more than that. You can be a god. You can figure out what's right and wrong for yourself. Come on. Take charge and make a difference! You'll be more important, more influential, more powerful. Do it, Eve. Take the step from being a creature under God to becoming an equal with God."

Blasphemous, isn't it? And yet, that was the temptation Eve fell for. Her next move was to play Junior Holy Spirit to Adam. She was the devil's best ally for taking Adam out.

The real thing

By the way, what is the work of the genuine Holy Spirit? It is fourfold.[2]

1. He convicts us of sin according to the principles of God's Word.
2. He points out the way of righteousness.
3. He calls us to make a decision.
4. He empowers us to do all He calls us to do.[3]

The Holy Spirit is the mightiest Power on earth, yet He never forces, never compels, never intimidates. He is potent yet polite; energetic yet gentle; strong yet sweet. To submit to His authority is to be restored to your own individuality, to be re-created in the image of God, to find the true glory of your manhood or womanhood.

God can bestow upon us no greater blessing than the gift of the Holy Spirit. He is spoken of as our down payment for the joys of heaven.[4] Why? Because He brings a little bit of heaven into our hearts. Remember the fruits of the Spirit—love, joy, peace, patience, kindness, goodness, faithfulness, gentleness, and self-control? What would it be like if that described your heart, your marriage, your family, your church, and your community? It would be heaven on earth, wouldn't it! Exactly!

But what happens when human beings try to take on themselves the office of the Holy Spirit and convict others of sin, telling them what they ought to do and trying to force them to submit? Just the opposite. Life becomes a hell that either smolders or burns with frenemy fire! And the

---

2. See John 16:8–11.
3. See Galatians 5:16.
4. See Ephesians 1:13, 14.

casualties continue to mount in our churches, families, and relationships.

What greater affront can we offer to God than to usurp the position of the One who has been appointed to restore and heal—and use that position to alienate and wound? Why do we fall for it? Why do we do it? We not only crush afresh the heart of our Savior, but we turn aside those whom He is drawing to Himself.

Why does the devil use Junior Holy Spirits to do the greatest damage? Why doesn't he use his worldly agents instead? Because He knows that Christians are best overcome by other Christians. He knows that the world can't defeat the church nearly as well as the church can defeat the church.

Some of you are saying, "No one has ever issued a fifty-page document against me. No one has tapped my phone, written me poison-pen letters, or cancelled my appointments."

For most, that may be true. But Junior Holy Spirits come in many packages.

Nonmoral issues

"Every fool will be meddling." A fool is one who is destitute of good sense and spiritual insight. In Scripture, a fool is one who follows his own inclinations and prefers to meddle in others' affairs rather than to know and follow the will of God.

Since that fateful day in the Garden, meddling has been something that comes naturally to our fallen natures. We meddle when we take it upon ourselves to interfere in the affairs of others. My grandmother called it being a busybody—sticking our noses in where they don't belong.

It makes me think of the *Red Skelton Show* on Sunday nights back in the early sixties. As I recall, Red would open almost every show with a mother-in-law joke.

I was mystified. "Mother, why is he always picking on Grandma? I don't get it."

My mother smiled knowingly. "Just wait a few years, Jimmie. You'll understand after you're married."

I can tell you honestly that when I married Christ, I began to find out what meddling was all about. These Junior Holy Spirits seem to think they can take the position of master over your conscience—tinkering and meddling and prescribing what you should and shouldn't do, even over nonmoral issues.

What is a nonmoral issue? It is one of those gray areas about which God has not given us a clear, precise, direct command. It is an area in which He works with us in our individuality and personality to apply His principles in ways that are best for us. We need to exercise toleration for one another in these areas—otherwise we very quickly become Junior Holy Spirits.

For example, it is a principle of Scripture that courtship for marriage should be characterized by purity and a sincere desire to honor God. But Scripture has given no precise command regarding the age when young people may begin contemplating the kind of person they should seek for a life partner.

When our sons, Matthew and Andrew, turned eighteen, we felt it was a reasonable time for them to begin considering girls. In our family discussions, we talked over the difference between worldly "dating around" and Christian courtship; the boys began to consider various girls in that context.

This was too much for some and almost scandalous for others. Gossip went around behind our backs. "Certainly a conservative family such as the Hohnbergers should set an example and not allow their boys to court until they're at least twenty-one!"

Is this a moral issue or a nonmoral issue? Is there a plain "Thus saith the Lord" on the age to begin courting? If I recall correctly, the young maiden God chose to be Jesus' mother was in her teens. Why do we put restrictions where God puts none?

One of these Junior Holy Spirits took it upon himself to warn a young lady my son was courting that my son wouldn't make a good husband because he was known to drive too fast. By this time, my son was in his early twenties and had been driving for seven years with no tickets or accidents. My son would never have known about this meddling except that the young lady had the courtesy to tell him. My son chose to have a courageous conversation with this person. I've often wondered how many tickets or accidents this "friend" had scored by the time he was the same age as my son!

It never ceases to amaze me what professed Christians find to meddle with.

"Jim, we understand that you take your family downhill skiing. Is that true?"

"Yes, it is."

"Well, we were visiting with the Sands the other day, and they mentioned that you do and that they have objections to it."

The Sands were a family we considered to be close friends. I was a bit surprised to hear this report.

"Oh really? Did they say why they thought that?"

"Well, no. But it made us kind of wonder."

After two different families approached us with this same report, I decided to have a courageous conversation with the Sands.

"Jim, you should know us better than that. You know we wouldn't say things like that behind your back. If we had a problem with you downhill skiing, we would tell you to your face."

They acted hurt that we would question them and seemed to feel that we were surmising evil. We apologized and dropped the subject.

But then a third family approached us and shared specific reasons that the Sands were against downhill skiing. "Jim, don't you know that the fashionable clothes worn on the slopes and in the lodges are a bad influence for our youth?"

"Well, perhaps. But if I take that as a principle, then I shouldn't allow my boys to go to a shopping mall, restaurant, or, for that matter, to church."

"But, Jim, you know that they play worldly music in the lodges and at the bottom of the chairlifts."

"I don't disagree with that, but we choose to eat in one of the lodges where no music is played. As for the few minutes we spend in line, I feel my boys are mature enough to deal with the music they hear there."

"Well, Jim, don't you think they charge too much for the lift tickets?"

"Yes, I do. But my boys have student passes that reduce the cost drastically."

"Well, the Sands and we think you need to set a better example."

This desire to prescribe someone else's duty based upon one's own personal perspective and preference is, to me, nothing less than being a Junior Holy Spirit. Have you done it? Are you doing it now to others?

When others approach me with a concern about an issue in someone else's life, the first thing I ask myself is, "Is this a moral issue or a nonmoral issue?" If there is no absolute "Thus saith the Lord" regarding the subject under discussion, it's a nonmoral issue, and we should leave it alone. I would venture to say that at least two-thirds of the problems I see in Christianity are due to self-appointed Junior Holy Spirits tinkering, meddling, and prescribing what everyone should or shouldn't do in almost every avenue of life.

In my opinion, the truly converted individual surrenders every inclination to be the Junior Holy Spirit in other peoples' lives. God has only one Holy Spirit, and it's not you or me. Stepping into His shoes is definitely a source of frenemy fire. It is not genuine Christianity; no, it's "Saulianity"—persecuting Christians as Saul did before he became the apostle Paul, persecuting others because they don't see everything the way we think they should.

Moral issues

What if the issue *is* a moral one—one for which we have a direct command of God, a clear, plain statement in the Scriptures? Should we just ignore violations of God's moral code? Should we allow the standards to be trampled upon? Are we not to speak up, stand for truth, and show God's people their sins? Certainly we are. But let's follow God's program and not our own. Even in moral issues, I find a real difference between being a Junior Holy Spirit and being the tool of the Holy Spirit.

In Matthew 18:15–17, God has laid down His way of handling moral issues: " 'If your brother sins against you, go and tell him his fault between you and him alone. If he hears you, you have gained your brother. But if he will not hear you, take with you one or two more, that "by the mouth of two or three witnesses every word may be established." And if he refuses to hear them, tell it to the church. But if he refuses even to hear the church, let him be to you like a heathen and a tax collector' " (NKJV.) In these verses, He gives us four steps to take.

First step

"If your brother sins against you, go and tell him his fault between you and him alone." Wow! What an injunction. First of all, God qualifies which moral issues we are to address—the ones that involve *us*. That includes those who have directly offended us as well as those within the sphere of our authority and influence. Some will be "under-responsible" and ignore issues they should address, while others will be "over-responsible" and take on dealing with situations in which they have no legitimate business. But when it becomes clear to you that there is a moral issue to address, note that God says, "Go! Go to the offending party and have a courageous conversation with that person *alone!*"

That, to me, is a major difference as to whether you are following God's Word or following your own inclination. You see, we can be a Junior Holy Spirit even when moral issues are involved. If I refuse to go to the offending party alone, but attack him in the public arena, instead, then I'm going against God. I'm a Junior Holy Spirit. God's program is very specific. "Go and tell him his fault between you and him *alone.*" But we don't do this very often. I'd say that in the vast majority of all cases, we violate God's Word while supposedly standing for His principles.

Why? I hear all sorts of excuses for not following God's instructions. "They won't listen." "I'm not gifted in speaking or reasoning." "They won't change." "I'm afraid." "They'll only make excuses." "I don't want to debate or argue." "It's not convenient." And so it goes.

As I read the Word of God, He just enjoins us to go. His instruction has nothing to do with our gifts or lack thereof. It has nothing to do with whether our brother will hear or forbear. It has nothing to do with whether it's easy or very, very hard. No, God just instructs us to go. If we don't do as He says, then *we* are in charge, and we are just as guilty as the party we are condemning.

The next steps

What if a courageous conversation doesn't resolve the issue? God gives a second step: " 'But if he will not hear, take with you one or two more, that "by the mouth of two or three witnesses every word may be established." ' "[5]

Wow! God wants to establish accountability. When you bring a witness—especially someone trained in the process of reconciliation—it's not just your word versus your brother's word. The neutral party can facilitate communication and ideally provide wisdom and guidance to restore the relationship—not just reprove the wrongdoer.

Many people have asked me, "Have you made up with your former associates?"

We have followed the first step of Jesus' counsel. We have met them alone for courageous conversations on multiple occasions, but we've

---

5. Matthew 18:16, NKJV.

found no resolution. We need to follow the second step, and I have since offered on several occasions to meet with them in the presence of a qualified reconciliation specialist, but they have declined to do so.

Seldom do I see or hear of someone following steps one or two in God's plan for dealing with the faults and deficiencies of His people. Why? Just ask yourself how many cases you've been involved with, or that you are aware of, where steps one and two have been followed. In the thirty years that I've been a Christian, I've seen hardly any.

God's third step is, " 'If he refuses to hear them, tell it to the church.' "[6] God is saying, "Take the issue to your community of members. Keep it contained to your local church, your institution, or your ministry of associates. Don't broadcast it to every itching ear and wagging tongue you run into. Don't try to win votes in a popular election. Take it to a confined body of associated believers—not for the purpose of splitting the body or dividing loyalties, but rather to increase accountability."

If the party in moral violation remains dug in, Christ's final instruction is to separate from them. " 'Let him be to you like a heathen and a tax collector.' "[7] This does not mean that we have a license to be unkind or heartless. Christ is our Model for how to treat the wrongdoer—always seeking to win the heart whether through blessings bestowed or blessings removed.

Now honestly, how often have you seen this biblical four-step process followed? I want to cry. I'm ashamed to give you my answer. No wonder God's people are destroying God's people. The blood is running through almost every church, ministry, and institution, yet real moral issues remain overlooked or poorly addressed. The Achans[8] in the camp remain undealt with, while the Moseses and Aarons are bleeding from attacks by the tinkerers, meddlers, and prescribers.[9]

As a result, the church is weak and ineffective. We bring people in the front door on facts, not faith, and many of them slip out the back door in less than a year. Why? Do you think it has anything to do with our mere mental assent to doctrinal dogma while we lack a true living experience of loving the brethren in word and deed? I do! If you and I

---

6. Verse 17, NKJV.

7. Ibid.

8. See Joshua 7.

9. See Exodus 15:24; 16:2; 17:3; Numbers 14:2.

refuse to follow these steps, then we are operating on our own. That's being a Junior Holy Spirit.

May God help us all—and that includes me. We *all* stand guilty! But we don't have to remain guilty. We can cease playing Junior Holy Spirit and learn, in God's wisdom and strength, to carry out His command for handling moral issues. His way is the only way. We need to follow Matthew 18:15–17.

It goes deeper yet

If we do manage to follow God's process for addressing moral issues, we still can become Junior Holy Spirits if our approach involves compulsion, force, manipulation, threats, a domineering attitude, politics, scare tactics, gossip, innuendos, or half-truths. God is interested in more than the correct form. He wants His Spirit and power to attend the entire process. It is very possible to follow a correct form while indulging a wrong spirit. It's called "having a form of godliness, but denying the power thereof."[10] The correct form without the restorative power of God's love, His principles, and His only Holy Spirit is useless.

A friend of mine calls this process the "steamroller." Do you get the picture? A steamroller compacts dirt, rock, or asphalt. Anything in its path gets mowed over and flattened. Have you ever been treated like that?

"We know better than you do. We're smarter than you are, more spiritual than you are, more righteous than you are. We are the voice of God to your soul. We know your sins, and you had better take our advice if you know what is good for you!"

God counsels, "From such turn away." Have nothing to do with ramrodding someone. Don't be a part of kangaroo courts or mock trials. They only hurt the cause of God and bring reproach upon His people. "From such turn away." Have nothing to do with them.

Whenever it is in your power, speak out against this approach, or you may become guilty of the sin of omission. Sure, you may not be a part of the steamroller, but have you used your voice and influence to stop the steamroller? Or have you folded your hands and shook your head as you watched it flatten your brother or sister?

This was Pilate's sin. He was too much of a coward to stand up to the

---

10. 2 Timothy 3:5.

band of Junior Holy Spirits when they were steamrolling Jesus. He thought he could wash his hands of it, but he was still accountable to God for his part in the injustice that was perpetrated upon an innocent Man when he said to them, "Take ye him, and crucify him: for I find no fault in him."[11]

Ohh! Ouch! Washing our hands and turning our backs on innocent blood! The sin of omission is failing to do what we know is right because it involves a cross. The person who remains silent is a coward and a traitor! From such a life turn away. May God forgive our silence as well as our misguided tongues!

Peter's dagger

Sometimes God would have us put both moral and nonmoral issues on the back burner. Sometimes there is more at stake than just upholding truth, biblical principles, and standards as we see them.

Now don't go shouting at me, "Liberal, liberal, liberal!" I'm very conservative in my theology and lifestyle, but I'm liberal in my approach to those who don't see things as I do. So was Jesus. He's the supreme Example, the perfect blend of conservative and liberal. He was balanced in everything. We need to look to Him—and Him only—for guidance as portrayed in His Word.

Now I have a question to ask: What would you have done with Peter's dagger? You remember Peter's dagger, don't you?

The disciples were with Jesus in the Garden of Gethsemane on the night of His betrayal. Peter was standing by His side. He had sworn he'd go to prison or to death for Jesus. Then Judas came on the scene, followed by a motley crowd, and betrayed Jesus into their hands with a kiss. The mob began to grab Jesus, and Peter was enraged. He grabbed his sword, or dagger, and went after the high priest's servant. I believe he was going for the servant's head, but missed and cut off his ear instead.

Was Peter acting as a Junior Holy Spirit here? Was he acting on his own impulse to defend the right? I think so.

Just for a moment, let's contrast Peter's actions with those of the One who had the genuine Holy Spirit. Jesus reached down, picked up the severed ear, and restored it completely to Malchus.[12] What a con-

11. John 19:6.
12. See John 18:10; Luke 22:51.

trast! Which example fits you—Peter's or Jesus'? Are you lopping off ears in the name of truth and righteousness? Or are you restoring the wounded under the influence of truth and the Holy Spirit?

What on earth was Peter doing running around with a dagger? Why hadn't Jesus had a courageous conversation with him regarding this fleshly weapon? These are honest, down-to-earth questions—questions we all need to ask ourselves. Isn't Peter's weapon a serious issue Jesus should have dealt with? Why didn't He?

To me, the answer is simple yet profound. It's the same answer to the question of why Jesus didn't address the woman at the well regarding her "dagger"—the six men in her life.[13] It's the same reason Jesus didn't address Judas about his "dagger"—stealing from the treasury.[14] It's the reason Jesus didn't address Simon about his "dagger"—his lack of courtesy when Jesus arrived for dinner.[15]

Why? Because it amounts to no saving good to get a person's "dagger" until you've gotten his heart. "Do you mean I need to win my brother's heart and not just his outward behavior?" you ask. "But it's his 'dagger' that bugs me! It's his 'dagger' that's offensive! It's his 'dagger' that I want to deal with! You mean I've got to deal with the heart?"

That's right! Once the heart is won, the individual gladly surrenders whatever "dagger" he has been hanging on to.

Well then, how are we supposed to know whether or not to address these issues? The answer is quite simple. If we are to address an issue, two elements must be in agreement—the Spirit and the truth.[16] We must follow the clear steps laid out in the Word of God, both for tolerating the perspectives of others on nonmoral issues and for dealing with moral issues. But more than that, we must come under the influence and guidance of the one true Holy Spirit in order to understand what is the proper approach and timing that can best facilitate restoration of the individual and relationship. It is an attitude and an approach that involves not only the letter of the law (truth), but also the Lord's present guidance in carrying it out (the Spirit).

"Well, Jim, that leaves me totally dependent not only upon the Word, but also upon God's Spirit guiding me in the correct use of His Word."

13. See John 4:7–26.
14. See John 12:6.
15. See Luke 7:36–50.
16. See John 4:23, 24.

Amen! Amen! Amen! And that brings us right back to the issue Eve faced at the tree of knowledge of good and evil when she succumbed to the temptation to become a Junior Holy Spirit: Who's in charge—God or us?

This is the downfall of so many self-righteous "do-gooders"—rebuking, chastising, and alienating others from the Savior rather than restoring and empowering them. May God spare us from not only religious intolerance but also from the mini-wars going on all over Christendom. May He help us to find genuine Christianity.

CHAPTER 8

JUNIOR HOLY SPIRITS

Questions to Consider for Personal Inventory or Group Discussions

1. Are you attempting to be a Junior Holy Spirit over others' consciences?
2. Do you tell the whole story, or are you a master of half-truths?
3. Are you consistently meddling in others' lives?
4. On moral issues, do you follow God's way of handling an offending brother or sister?
   Step 1. Go and tell him his fault between you and him alone.
   Step 2. If he will not hear you, take with you one or two other individuals.
   Step 3. If he still refuses to hear, tell the issue to the church.
   Step 4. Finally, if he continues to refuse to listen, separate from him.
5. Honestly, how often have you seen or followed this biblical four-step process?
6. Does your approach involve compulsion, force, manipulation, threats, a domineering attitude, or scare tactics?
7. Have you ever been "steamrolled," or have you "steamrolled" others?
8. Have you ever washed your hands and turned your back on innocent blood?
9. What would you have done about Peter's "dagger"?
10. Do you recognize the difference between moral, nonmoral, and personal conscience issues?

Genuine Christianity

In Him we live, and move, and have our being.
—Acts 17:28

This was the third time I had taken my vehicle to the service department for the same problem—a clunking sound somewhere under the driver's seat! It was a nuisance. No, it was more than a nuisance. It was a nagging thorn in my side.

I had taken in my vehicle for repair twice before—and both times the repairman had told me he couldn't find anything wrong. Yet the clunking noise remained. Why couldn't it be fixed? Soon, my warranty would expire, and then the bill would be on me.

The temptation tugged at me to feel impatient with these guys. Their nonchalant attitude went directly against my grain. My pet peeve is inefficiency. I like to see things done right the first time—on time! I was sure hoping the repair shop would get it right the third time around!

Throughout this process, I had made several phone calls to the service department and invariably had been put on hold for five, ten, fifteen—even twenty minutes. I left messages for the service manager to call me back, and he rarely got around to it. I was not pleased with the service. Surely today the repairman would redeem himself by finding the problem and fixing it promptly.

My appointment was scheduled for 1:00 P.M. I arrived at 12:40 and signed in my vehicle.

"As I told you on the phone, Jerry," I told the service manager, "I hear the 'clunk' right under the driver's seat. Take a look there, and I think you'll find the problem."

"Don't worry about a thing, Jim," he replied amiably. "We'll get right on it."

I glanced out the window and saw Andrew, my son, just pulling in to pick up Sally and me for lunch. "I'll be back after two-thirty, Jerry," I said. "You've got my cell-phone number if you need to go over something with me, right?"

"I sure do, Jim. We'll see you in a bit."

Christianity is revealed in a crisis

Two and a half hours later, I came back. As I approached the service desk, I noticed through the window behind the service manager that my vehicle had just been driven into the garage.

Uh-oh! I thought.

"Are you just now getting to my vehicle?" I asked as Jerry looked up.

"Yes, sir. I don't know why, but I'll check on it."

I wanted to explode! *What is wrong with these people? What kind of an operation is this?* I had been early for my scheduled appointment and then had allowed an extra forty-five minutes at the end of the appointment—and still the mechanic hadn't even touched my car! The unfairness, the lack of professionalism, and the ineptness was really getting under my skin! I didn't have time to stand around for another hour and a half waiting for my car to be fixed.

My flesh wanted to become a one-man firing squad. Let them have both barrels. Put them in their place. Steamroll them with a good piece of my mind. *I'm right. They're wrong. I have the right to unleash on them, don't I?*

I saw the look in the service manager's eyes. I was sure he'd been on the receiving end of this scenario numerous times. He knew his employees were wrong.

So what should a Christian do? Give them a verbal blast? Storm out of the building and never come back? March into the owner's office and carry on a tirade? Withdraw into the "icy pricklies" and give them a cold shoulder? Have a pity party?

Not only was my flesh speaking to me, but God was also speaking through my conscience. *"Let all bitterness, wrath, anger, clamor, and evil speaking be put away from you, with all malice. And be kind to one another, tenderhearted, forgiving one another, just as God in Christ also forgave you."* [1]

"Be kind, Lord? Tenderhearted? Forgive them when they are so inept—three times in a row?"

I knew what was right. But my flesh was drawing me into a tyranny far worse than the frustration of the circumstances. I've tasted that tyranny before—far too many times. I didn't want it, yet it demanded I yield to it. "Just say a few choice words to put them in their place, Jim, and then your flesh will be satisfied, and you can go back to being a Christian."

Does your flesh lie to you the way mine does to me? I needed a time-out. I told the service manager I'd be back and stepped out the door. Taking a deep breath, I started down the sidewalk.

"Give it to Me, Jim. Let Me temper your disposition. I will give you rest. I will guide you in your choice of words. It won't solve anything to lash out and demand your rights. Let it go, Jim."

The real test

I've heard it said that we do most of our sinning when we are "right." Think about that for a moment. For many, Christianity is about being "right"—right doctrines, right reforms, right diet, and right lifestyle. They live and move and have their being in their "rightness." And when someone else doesn't do it right, or think it right, or go about it right, these Christians become Junior Holy Spirits and set out to correct them, to convert them to their "rightness." This is the basis for most of the religious intolerance—frenemy fire—recorded in history and carried on in the present day.

The Jews persecuted the Christians because the Jews were "right." The Inquisition was carried on because the Mother Church was "right." The Crusades were conducted because the crusaders were "right." The Irish Catholics and Protestants set off bombs against each other because each believed they were "right." Jihadists of all stripes make their ugly smear against humanity because they are "right."

---

1. Ephesians 4:31, 32, NKJV.

God save us from being "right"!

Now there is no question that correct doctrine, reforms, and lifestyle have their proper place. They are part of the blessing that comes with genuine Christianity. But they are not the *test* of genuine Christianity. Jesus gave us one test of real Christianity: " 'By this all will know that you are My disciples, if you have love for one another.' "[2]

Why is love for each other the test? Because we can't generate it ourselves. We can generate "rightness." We can use logic to make our way to correctness. But no one can manufacture genuine principled love that suffers long and is still kind, that bears all things, believes all things, hopes all things, and endures all things while not enabling iniquity.[3]

This kind of love comes *only* from God and finds expression in our lives *only* to the extent that we yield to the principles of His Word and the influence of the Holy Spirit, allowing Him to shed His love abroad in our hearts.[4]

As I walked down the sidewalk—my flesh smoking, needing only the spark of my choice to ignite it into frenemy fire—I realized that I could choose to live and move and have my being in my "rightness" or in Christ. Who would be in charge—Jim Hohnberger or Christ?

Jesus came to free us! Not from the inconveniences caused by others. Not from wrong treatment or the injustices of life. Jesus came to free us on the inside, from our own temperament. To bring us a peace in the midst of our storms—whether these storms are out-and-out attacks against our families and ourselves or the negligent fumbling of a service department.

I sensed God's call to my heart. His grace was speaking to my conscience. It was a still, small Voice asking me to allow Christ to be first, last, and best in my life, in my day, in this present situation. *"Choose you this day whom ye will serve."*[5]

I made my decision. "I want to live and move and have my being in You, Lord. I relinquish my right to be 'right.' What would You have me to do, Lord?"

---

2. John 13:35, NKJV.
3. See 1 Corinthians 13:4–7.
4. See Romans 5:5.
5. Joshua 24:15.

"Jim, I'd like you to have a courageous conversation with the service manager."

"Lord, my flesh is still chomping at the bit. Are You sure I'm safe to begin a courageous conversation right now?"

"Jim, just keep yielding those impulses to Me moment by moment, and I'll keep supplying you the grace and the words you need moment by moment. That's how I live in you the way the Father lived in Me."[6]

This was a call to act on faith—a faith that cooperates with His grace in the moment. A faith that says, "Yes, Lord. You can be in charge, and I willingly surrender being in charge. Yes, Lord, I will honor You and depend upon You for the words and disposition to do as You ask." This is genuine Christianity. It is allowing Christ to have me fully, every moment of every hour of every day.

It has nothing to do with seeking fairness, justice, or my rights. It has nothing to do with gritting my teeth to keep the flesh from finding expression. It has everything to do with allowing Christ's life to flow into my being and for self to die. It is saying "yes" to God and "no" to self.

The choice less chosen

I returned to the service desk.

"Jerry, I'm sorry, but I really don't have enough time left in my schedule today to wait another hour and a half. Could you please have your mechanic bring my vehicle to the front door?"

Jerry stared at me, confusion written on his face. I could sense him wondering, *Is that it? No retaliation? Isn't this guy going to spit at me? Threaten me?* He was waiting for more, but no more came.

"In him we live, and move, and have our being"[7]—that's freedom, real freedom!

Jerry hurried into the garage to get my vehicle while I stepped out the front door where Andrew was waiting with Sally to transfer a pressure sprayer from his vehicle to mine. After making the transfer, I thanked Andrew and asked him and Sally to pray for me while I returned to the service department.

---

6. See John 17:21.
7. Acts 17:28.

This time Jerry was not there. Instead, a harried-looking woman was busying herself with a stack of papers. "Ma'am, I would like to see the service manager."

"You'll just have to wait until I finish this paperwork," she snapped back rudely.

Ouch! That was another slam. *What's with these people today?* I asked myself. *This is supposed to be a five-star dealership where service is number one.*

"Jim, they need to see genuine Christianity lived out—not preached, but lived in shoes, your shoes, today, here, now."

I walked over to the service manager's door and looked through the window. The desk manager, the service manager, and the mechanic were having a powwow. I was sure it was about my situation, so I knocked on the door. The service manager motioned for me to come in.

As I stepped into the room, I could sense their apprehension. All three pairs of eyes had a look of dread in them—the fear that this thing could explode. They were bracing themselves for the hailstorm they were sure was about to begin. After all, they knew they had blown it three times in a row. Yes, they knew they were in for it.

"Guys, I'm not very happy right now," I began honestly. I wasn't stuffing my irritation down. I was willing to own it and surrender it to Christ. "This is my third trip in here. But I'm not going to focus on my irritation. I just want to solve this situation."

God calls us to be proactive—not reactive. He wants to lead us to solutions, not leave us wallowing in the problems. Christianity says we can live above the situation. We don't have to allow provocation, injustice, or foul play to dictate how we live and move and have our being. No, Calvary not only has freed us from our past life of reactive living but it has also empowered us to find a proactive response.

The atmosphere relaxed slightly.

Jerry looked over at Ron, the mechanic. "What do you think could be causing that noise?"

Ron took a deep breath, squirmed in his chair, and frowned. "It's hard to say, Jerry. It could be caused by a cracked torsion bar. If that's the case, we'll have to pull it from the vehicle and send it off to Wright's Welding to be repaired. That could take at least two days."

The torsion bar. I knew that ran down the middle of my car and tied the front of the frame to the back. The only place it could possibly create a clunking sound would be to my right and behind me when I'm sitting in the driver's seat.

"I don't think it's there, guys. The sound is coming from under my foot when I step on the brakes—not from behind me in the center of the car."

Terry the desk manager interjected, "Could it be a loose exhaust pipe or muffler? What about the muffler brackets?"

"No," I replied. "I've pushed and prodded on all that stuff, and the noise isn't coming from there."

The three men were still sitting there nervously, waiting for the explosion. They were grabbing at any idea they could come up with to pacify me.

"Lord," I breathed silently, "this is ridiculous! How are You ever going to bring good out of this?" My flesh still wanted to let them have it!

"Jim, will unleashing on them fix your car? Do you want to live and move and have your being in Me with a clunky car or would you rather live and move and have your being in your 'rightness,' your flesh, and your emotions—with a clunky car?"

"Lord, I want to stay in You—clunky car or not."

Ron suddenly blurted out, "If you've got just five minutes, I'll put your vehicle on the drive-in rack and let you look underneath it with all of us."

Wow! I wasn't expecting that! The insurance policies of these places do not permit customers under the vehicles. I kind of wondered what good it would do, but it seemed God was moving on their hearts now, not just my own.

I handed Ron the keys. "Let's give it a try!"

A few moments later, we were all standing beneath my vehicle. The tension had relaxed even more, and we were starting to work as a team. We poked around a bit and found nothing out of place. Then Jerry got an idea. Grabbing the back bumper, he rocked my vehicle up and down. Ron grabbed hold under the front bumper. My vehicle looked like a ship on a choppy sea—rocking up and down, back and forth.

All of a sudden I heard the clunk—very softly, but distinctly. "There it is!" I exclaimed.

They all crowded around to look. Sure enough, the left front tie-rod was loose. We were all elated.

Jerry slapped me on the back. "Jim, you're hired!"

I grinned back at him and joked, "For how much?"

"For whatever you want!"

They lowered the vehicle, ordered the replacement part, and scheduled appointment number four. Jerry and Ron walked me out to my vehicle. All the coolness was replaced now with a sense of camaraderie. We were a team—not enemies. They chatted good-naturedly with Sally and wished us a good afternoon.

I drove off thinking about Acts 17:28. *"In him we live, and move, and have our being."* That's genuine Christianity. The kind of Christianity the world is waiting to see in your life and my life—daily, hourly, moment by moment. The kind of Christianity in which principled love seeks solutions, not merely Band-Aids.

I reflected on how different the scenario would have been if I had not chosen to respond to my Savior's call upon my heart. My initial thoughts flashed back into my mind. What if I had chosen to simply react to their ineptness? We'd all have been losers.

Can one person make a difference? What would happen in our marriages if just one spouse would begin to follow the Savior's call to his or her heart? How different would our families be if the parents lived such a life?

Genuine Christianity is taking the choice rarely made. It is making the decision to say, "God, You are in charge. I'll surrender my rights and allow Your Spirit to flow through me, now and always. I want to live to honor You in all the circumstances of life."

In Him

I am coming to see that it isn't enough to merely be in a church, in a lifestyle, in a work, or in our truths. Genuine Christianity goes the full distance and allows us to be *in Him*—and He in us. To have most of the above and not be in Him every day, throughout our day, is to have the outward form while lacking the inward power.[8]

---

8. See 2 Timothy 3:5.

God offers us power daily to become His sons and daughters.[9] When I consent to let God live out His life in me in the moment, I experience a genuine Christianity that goes beyond the form and grasps the substance of the real gospel. It saves me from myself. More than a mere clerical notation of my name in the books of heaven, it empowers my life where the rubber meets the road. It's appropriating His grace by faith through a surrender of my will, my choice, my thoughts and emotions, all motivated by a love for God—not the hope of a reward or the fear of punishment.

I would serve my God even if He told me there was no heaven. I don't follow Him for what's in it for me. That would be selfishness. I follow Him because of what He's done for me. He's caused me to fall in love with Him—not with His perks. As a byproduct of that love, He will grant me eternal life. My focus is on Him—not on me.

He wants to dwell in me and for me to dwell in Him. He wants to put His Spirit in me to enable me to live and move and have my being in Him.[10] That's what was happening at the service desk. God was allowing circumstances to arise that would give me an opportunity to learn how to live and move and have my being in Him.

Practice makes perfect. That's why God allows unfairness, disappointment, injustice, and frenemy fire to touch our lives. Every time it does, we are to hear a call to genuine Christianity where self is subdued and His life flows through us. We are either in Christ or out of Christ. When we are in Christ—that is genuine Christianity. The fruit of the Spirit within us will be seen in all goodness, righteousness, and truth, regardless of circumstances. When we call ourselves "Christian," but are out of Christ—that is professed Christianity. The weaknesses of our fallen nature control us whenever circumstances call forth that nature.

Ready or not?

The Bible calls a professed Christianity being a "foolish virgin." You remember the story Jesus told His disciples.[11] Ten young maidens—

9. See John 1:12.
10. See Acts 17:28.
11. See Matthew 25:1–13.

virgins—went out to meet the bridegroom. They all had lamps and vessels for oil, and they were all eager for the wedding. Jesus said that five of them were wise and five were foolish. At first glance, you wouldn't know which was which—until the crisis hit.

There was a delay—sort of like my delay at my vehicle's service center. Things didn't go as these girls had planned, and then you saw the difference. The wise virgins had extra oil, but the foolish did not. The wise allowed the Spirit to have complete reign in their affairs, but the foolish fumbled in their own resources.

What about you? When your expectations are disappointed, when someone crosses your pet peeve, or when circumstances take a sharp turn, do you possess the oil of the Spirit to keep your lamp brightly burning? Or are you a foolish virgin?

Let me ask it another way. Are you dead while your life is hid with Christ in God?[12] Can you say with Paul, "I am crucified with Christ: nevertheless I live; yet not I, but Christ liveth in me: and the life which I now live in the flesh, I live by the faith of the Son of God, who loved me, and gave Himself for me"?[13] To be crucified with Christ means you consent for all the irritation at the bungling of the service department to be laid aside and to treat those who have let you down—not as they deserve, but as God has treated you.

Jesus died to give us life. We must die to receive His life. That's why Paul declared, "I die daily."[14] Dying daily to our fallen natures is what allows God to work through us to demonstrate to the service department, and to the world, genuine Christianity.

This daily experience is greatly lacking in professed Christianity today. Part of the reason is that we don't understand how it works, and yet this "in Christ" experience is available to all, every day, regardless of our past, irrespective of our present. It has nothing to do with our religious affiliation. We are all His children. God pours His grace out on the heathen as well as on the Christian, on the sinner and the saint alike. Whether you are a Catholic, Orthodox Jew, Protestant, liberal, conservative, or atheist, God is there for you—offering you His grace.

---

12. See Colossians 3:3.
13. Galatians 2:20.
14. 1 Corinthians 15:31.

Appropriated grace—a continuous call

"By grace you have been saved through faith, and that not of your-selves; it is a gift of God, not of works, lest anyone should boast."[15]

Grace is "unmerited favor." That's the theological term, and it is cor-rect. However, for years I wrestled with what that means in a practical way when I am overwhelmingly provoked at a bungling service counter. What does "unmerited favor" mean to me when irritation is oozing out of every fiber of my being?

When we first moved to the mountains of Montana more than twenty years ago, one of the big questions in my mind was *how* Enoch walked with God. If he could walk with God, why couldn't I? "God, I'd like to sit at Enoch's feet and learn how to walk with You the way he did."

"Jim, how about if I teach you Myself how to walk with Me?"

"You teach me? Personally? Is that possible?"

"I will instruct thee and teach thee in the way which thou shalt go; I will guide thee with mine eye."[16]

So I began to study God's Word under the direction of His Spirit. Everywhere I turned, I saw that God is present with us always. He never leaves us nor forsakes us. When Daniel faced the den of lions, God was there. When the three Hebrews were tossed into the fiery fur-nace, God was there. When Joshua faced Jericho, God was there. He was always there to save His people in the present. The Scriptures say we are saved by grace, yet it is evident to me that God is the One who saves.

And so, over the years, an experiential definition of *grace* has been distilled in my mind. It is this: God's presence goes with us every mo-ment of every hour of every day, wooing us, entreating us, and beckon-ing us. He is trying to save us in the present, in the here and the now, that He may guide us, direct us, empower us, redeem us, and restore us. This divine influence is unmerited. We have done nothing to deserve it. We can't earn it. It is simply a daily gift from God, who makes His grace available to everyone—even the chief of sinners whom I see my-self to be.

---

15. Ephesians 2:8, 9, NKJV.
16. Psalm 32:8.

Most of us resist this divine influence upon our hearts, and that's why we remain foolish virgins. You see, in order for grace to be effective in our lives, we must respond to it. We must appropriate it.

God's grace was there to save me from blowing my top in the dealership garage, but I had to choose to cooperate with it. I had to surrender my thoughts and embrace what God was asking me to do and not succumb to what my flesh was dictating. "There is therefore now no condemnation to those who are in Christ Jesus, who do not walk according to the flesh, but according to the Spirit."[17] That kind of effort is not legalism. Legalism is trying to do it all in our own willpower, apart from grace. It's an entirely different kind of effort.

From our side of the equation, salvation is a choice, an appropriating of this divine gift into our lives in the moment. God has made us all free moral agents. He supplies the grace, the power, and the wisdom. We simply have to choose to cooperate with it.

From the divine side, salvation is a pursuit, an apprehending, and a conquest of our complete hearts by our long-suffering God. He's given all of Himself. All He asks in return is all of ourselves—all our known choices.

God initiates. We can only respond.[18] That's what makes it all a gift. That's why God is called the "author and finisher of our faith."[19] Thus, grace is a divine influence upon our hearts—daily, hourly, moment by moment—in order to allow Him to be seen, and not us. But will we appropriate this grace?

Connecting faith—a continuous response
Faith is not only a belief in God's Word, but also a continuous dependence upon Him in every circumstance. It is a surrender of my known choices to Him in the moment that He may enable me to live as He would. It connects me to the One who is able to supply all the wisdom and power I need to live the life I was created to live.

As I stood before the service manager, I was irate. How could he do this to me? At that point I was like a disabled vehicle needing to be

17. Romans 8:1, NKJV.
18. See John 6:44.
19. Hebrews 12:2.

pulled out of the ditch of self-pity and self-importance. God is like the tow truck. He has the power to lift me up and out of the old ditch I know only too well. Faith is the tow strap that connects the disabled vehicle with the enabling vehicle. I can choose to hook up. There is no cost for the tow. It's all free. I've done nothing to earn it or deserve it. But if I don't appropriate this grace, of my own free will, I will remain disabled. All the while I may be claiming to have a pure doctrine, I might be going to the right church and perhaps even helping others to know about the great God of heaven. And yet, if I do not cooperate with and possess this grace, it all amounts to no saving good. It's available! It's free! But I remain a disabled vehicle unless I hook up.

It is said of Christ, "In the morning, having risen a long while before daylight, He went out and departed to a solitary place; and there He prayed."[20] He hooked up. He connected with the Source of His power. He never relied upon His own wisdom and strength. He even declared, "I can of mine own self do nothing."[21] Jesus chose to live life just as you and I have to—always dependent upon His Father for wisdom and power and guidance. As Jesus was, so are we to be—always dependent through an active, living faith to appropriate His grace in the here and now. [22] That's genuine Christianity.

Grace, then, is a continuous call from God, while faith is our continuous response to God. They go together in the same way that hydrogen and oxygen form H_2O, or water. Without both hydrogen and oxygen, you do not have water. Without both faith and grace, you are merely a professed Christian. But when faith responds to grace, and unites with grace, you are a genuine Christian, or as the Bible says, a wise virgin. Why? Because you have not only a profession but also an appropriation.

Opening the gift

My wife loves to receive gifts. And I love to give them to her—not because she earns it (although her value truly is far above rubies), but simply because I love her. One of her favorite gifts is flowers.

---

20. Mark 1:35, NKJV.
21. John 5:30.
22. See 1 Peter 2:21.

Suppose I bought her a box of one hundred Holland tulip bulbs, and I bought them in the autumn season at the right time for her to plant them in her flower bed for next spring. I imagine how much fun she is going to have when she opens the gift, plants the bulbs, and then watches for them to pop up and bloom when the snow melts. Her garden is going to be absolutely vibrant with living color! I wrap the gift up with the prettiest paper I can find, top it with a frilly bow, and write a little love note to go with it. Then I wait for just the right moment to give it to her. I can't wait to see her face when she opens it!

Her eyes open wide with surprise and pleasure. "Why, Jim! That's the prettiest present I've ever been given!"

She reads the love note and gives me a big hug and kiss. "Oh, Jim! You are so thoughtful, and I love you so much! I am going to treasure this gift for the rest of my life! I'm going to look at it and admire it every day! Thank you so much! I can't wait to tell all my friends about this lovely gift!"

And then she takes the gift, all wrapped and lovely, and sticks it on the top shelf of her closet.

Can you imagine how disappointed I would feel? Sure, she is grateful for the gift—but she didn't open it! She will never know what I really gave her or enjoy the full potential that could be hers if she would only open the gift.

Grace is a beautiful gift. God is the Giver. He has put within that gift the potential for greater beauty than we can imagine, and He can't wait to see it blooming in our lives. But we must open it. Can you imagine how He feels when we receive the gift of His grace, admire it, talk about it, write sermons on it, tell others about it, thank Him for it—but never open it? Unless we appropriate it in our thoughts, feelings, and responses to life, we will never realize what it truly is or the beauty God means to bring into our lives through it.

God is no respecter of persons. He gives to all according to their need. Even the impulse to open the gift originates with God, yet it remains with us to exercise that impulse in the moment. God was giving freely of His grace to me in that service department, but His gift would have done me no saving good without my response of faith—unless I opened the gift.

In other words, grace first—then faith. God's part is always first.

Our part is always second. He invites. We respond. " 'No one can come to Me unless the Father who sent Me draws him.' "[23] I'm learning how to recognize the call of God upon my heart and then to cooperate with Him.[24] God is always calling. His presence is always with us.[25] Will we consent to allow Him in?

All of this is what Paul summarizes as the "in Christ" experience. "There is therefore now no condemnation to those who are in Christ Jesus, who do not walk according to the flesh, but according to the Spirit."[26] This entire process liberates us from our sin and selfishness of the past and the constant temptations of the devil and the flesh in the present.

One question

Who's in charge? Are you, or is God? In my opinion, that is the entire issue from the book of Genesis to the book of Revelation. Are you going to allow God in—fully, completely—or are you going to be in charge? With Lucifer, it started out as a simple thought—then grew into all out war. He convinced Adam to join Him in His rebellion—this disposition to be in charge.

The gospel isn't complicated. It's very, very simple. You have inherited a fallen nature that wants to run the show. God wants to give you a new nature. It's the great exchange—His goodness and righteousness, His wisdom and power, for your selfishness and ineptness. He offers this to you every day. He wants to free you—not merely pardon you. He "is able to keep you from stumbling, and to present you faultless before the presence of His glory with exceeding joy."[27]

That's my God! That's your God! That's what grace abounding to the chief of sinners is all about. Faith connects me and sets me free to live above frenemy fire. Free to be hit again and again, yet empowered to lay aside every hit, every slight, every indignation and the hurt that so easily besets me and to run with patience the "Y. A. C. yards" that are before me!

---

23. John 6:44, NKJV.
24. See Isaiah 30:21.
25. See Hebrews 13:5.
26. Romans 8:1, NKJV.
27. Jude 24.

Chapter 9

═══ Genuine Christianity ═══

Questions to Consider for Personal Inventory or Group Discussions

1. Are you easily agitated and annoyed when things don't go your way?
2. Do you vent your irritation?
3. Do you stuff down the things that annoy you and stew over them?
4. Are you able to work out a solution with those who treat you unfairly?
5. Are you proactive or reactive?
6. Are you solution-oriented or problem-driven?
7. Would your spouse, family, and friends say you are "in Christ" or "in self"?
8. Are you a "wise virgin" or a "foolish virgin"?
9. Do you recognize the call of grace to your heart throughout your day?
10. Do you appropriate God's grace daily?
11. Do you consistently surrender your will to God's will and depend upon Him for wisdom and power?
12. Is your focus to please Jesus or to gain the reward of heaven and eternal life?
13. Who's truly in charge in your life?

Y. A. C. Yards

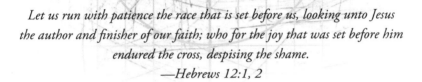

Let us run with patience the race that is set before us, looking unto Jesus the author and finisher of our faith; who for the joy that was set before him endured the cross, despising the shame.
—Hebrews 12:1, 2

It was fourth down, with one minute and forty-three seconds to go. The opposing team was ahead seventeen to thirteen. We were on their twenty-third yard line. A field goal would still leave us behind by one point. We needed a touchdown! I was sixteen years old and playing left halfback on the Appleton High School junior varsity team.

The coach called, "Time-out!" We all huddled around him, breathing heavily, feeling the tension of the moment. The coach glanced around at our grim faces and then his eyes locked with mine.

"Hohnberger, it's up to you! Don't stop until you cross the end zone."

My eyes got big. My mouth went dry. My heart started pounding. Why did he call on me? I was only 5' 10" and 150 pounds. Why not send in our fullback at 6' 2" and 195 pounds? Quickly scanning the sidelines, I could make out the faces of my friends, parents, and girl-friend, who were cheering us on to victory. The honor of our team was at stake. We couldn't disappoint them. I thought about the opposing team. Some of them were pretty big and burly. The pressure was mounting. This was big-time stuff. I was nervous!

Y. A. C. Yards after contact. When they hit you from the side, when they grab you by the jersey, when they come at you from behind, when they double-team you head-on, do you keep on going, or do you fall to the ground? Do you keep running for daylight, or do you allow them to take you down?

We took our places at the line of scrimmage. The quarterback called the play—a left-hand sweep. He tossed the ball to me. Tucking it under my arm, I ran with all I had—determined, excited, and fearful all at the same moment. Suddenly, I was hit from the side. I spun around, but kept going, my legs pumping me forward. Someone grabbed my jersey, but I plowed ahead. My eyes were on the end zone, and nothing was going to stop me. Between me and it waited two of the biggest brutes I'd ever seen. They looked like Goliath with a glare that threatened, "You're stopping here!" Quickly noting my possible routes, I decided to dash right between them. They lunged at me, made contact, and hung on. I staggered momentarily, but I could see the goal line. It was only a few feet away now!

Keep going, Hohnberger! I pushed myself. *Don't buckle under the weight! Don't stop! Don't give in! Move those legs! Come on, move those legs! Don't go down!*

My muscles were exhausted, my lungs burned, my legs threatened to crumple under the weight of those two linebackers. But I wasn't going to give in!

When I hit the ground with sweaty bodies piled on top of me, I was just inches *over* the end zone. Touchdown!

I can't tell you the exhilaration you feel when you know you have faced overwhelming odds and didn't buckle. You stood the test. You did your best. You gave it your all, and you crossed the finish line. You didn't just survive—you thrived!

God's boot camp

How about you? Are you being hit from behind? Are they charging you from the side? Are they tackling you head-on? Are they grabbing at your jersey, jerking on your face mask, or piling on top of you? Unfortunately, all this is part of life. It's also part of the Christian walk. "All who desire to live godly in Christ Jesus will suffer persecution."[1]

If your Coach is God and you are listening to His instructions, you will run into linebackers determined to stop you. If your eyes are on the

---

1. 2 Timothy 3:12, NKJV.

end zone, you can expect to be tackled. If you are putting your all into finishing the race of life to His glory, you will be hit. Being hit may cause you to spin around or stumble, but don't let it take you down.

Keep your eyes on the goal. The goal is not to exonerate yourself. It is not to prove your frenemies all wrong and yourself all right. It is not to find a happy ending to your sad story. The goal is to finish the work your heavenly Coach has assigned you—just like Jesus did. His death on the cross bore the appearance of cruel defeat when, in reality, He had just made a touchdown. He had glorified God and finished the work that had been given Him to do.[2] At every step, from the manger to the tomb, He had done His Father's will and not His own. At every step He was hit by opposition, but His yards after contact took Him over the end zone with the triumphant cry, "It is finished"![3]

The very resistance calculated to destroy Him proved to be rungs on a ladder by which He climbed to victory.[4] The very brutes that intended to block my course to the end zone proved to be the ones who made my triumph so exhilarating. The very circumstances pressing you down into despair can be the vehicle for your greatest success. God does not want you just to survive life with a mediocre character. He wants you to thrive by overcoming obstacles and pressing through difficulties. He wants you to be able to say, "That was the best thing that ever happened to me in the worst possible way!"

It's part of God's program. Without trials, we don't recognize our need of Him. Without conflict, we don't realize our great weakness. Without opposition, the gold of our faith mingles with the dross of self-reliance. We become spiritual couch potatoes and Monday morning quarterbacks instead of running our race with endurance.

Therefore, God calls us from the sidelines and says, "It's up to you. No one can fill your place in the game of life. My honor is at stake in your life. Don't stop until you reach the end zone." He sends us out on the field with a goal. He allows us to be challenged to the depths of our souls. He permits the enemy to tackle us from every angle until we become strong in faith and fixed in purpose. He develops our Y. A. C. yards.

---

2. See John 17:4.
3. John 19:30.
4. See 2 Peter 1:2–8.

God's fullback

On the dusty road to Damascus, God called Paul—not from the sidelines, but from the opposition—and commissioned him to run. Paul caught sight of the goal and never turned aside from it. He fervently states, "I have suffered the loss of all things, and do count them but dung, that I may win Christ, and be found in him, not having mine own righteousness, which is of the law, but that which is through the faith of Christ . . . that I may know him, and the power of his resurrection, and the fellowship of his sufferings. . . . I press toward the mark for the prize of the high calling of God in Christ Jesus."[5] His purpose was fixed, his aim set, his eye single.

Do you suppose he ran his course without opposition? Of course not! His entire missionary career was a gauntlet dogged by envious Jews determined to take him out. But Paul's yards after contact were incredible.[6]

Opposed in Antioch, he and Barnabas "shook off the dust of their feet against them, and came to Iconium."[7] In Iconium, he ran head-on into the unbelieving Jews who stirred up the Gentiles and poisoned their minds against him. But Paul stayed his ground speaking "boldly in the Lord."[8] Finally, a violent attempt was made on his life, and he fled to Lystra—not as a coward, but as one with his eyes on the prize.

In Lystra, Paul healed a man who had been crippled from his mother's womb, and the crowds began to flock to him. Then the Jews from Antioch and Iconium came there and persuaded the multitudes to turn against Paul and Barnabas. In a few hours, the fickle mob that had been ready to worship Paul and Barnabas as gods turned against them and stoned Paul. Assuming he was dead, they dragged him out of the city and dumped him there.

But did that stop Paul? No! He rose up and went back into the city! Talk about yards after contact! No man in his right mind would do that! But Paul did. Why? Because he was looking to Jesus—not the conflict, not the hurt, not the sorrow. Jesus was his focus. Paul's life shows there can be joy and peace in running with endurance the race that is set before us.

---

5. Philippians 3:8–14.
6. See Acts 13, 14.
7. Acts 13:51, NKJV.
8. Acts 14:3.

What are you thinking right now? What is the Holy Spirit whispering to you? How do your Y. A. C. yards stack up to Paul's?

Leaving Lystra, Paul and Barnabas moved on to Derbe. When Paul had preached the gospel in that city and made many disciples, he returned to Lystra, Iconium, and Antioch, strengthening the souls of the disciples, exhorting them to continue in the faith and saying, "We must through many tribulations enter the kingdom of God."[9]

Tribulations! We must go through *many tribulations* in order to reach the end zone? That's what it says. All who live godly in Christ Jesus will stir up the envy and jealousy of the "saints." They will experience—along with Jesus and Paul—trial and suffering with not always an instant victory. God does not promise that the Christian life will be without struggle. Giving our lives over to Christ and living for Him does not preempt all suffering. In fact, it almost always assures it in one form or another.

Joseph was sold-out by his own brothers and, later, by the master he had served faithfully. Moses was the meekest man on earth, and yet the people to whom he had devoted his life repeatedly turned against him. Isaiah spent his lifetime as a patient, courageous teacher—a prophet of hope as well as of doom. Yet he was snubbed and ignored by many in Israel, and according to tradition was sawn in half at the hands of Manasseh. Jeremiah worked tirelessly to save Judah from doom and was rewarded by being lowered with cords into a muddy pit. And "Jeremiah sunk in the mire."[10]

Elijah was called the "troubler" of Israel.[11] Zechariah, the son of Jehoiada the priest, was stoned in the temple for daring to sound a call to repentance.[12] Virtually, all the disciples died a martyr's death. Examine the lives of the Reformers. Wycliffe, Huss, Jerome, Luther, Zwingli, and Wesley all faced persecution of one kind or another. Every one of them was tested to the core. Every one of them faced moments of discouragement. Every one of them was tempted to give up and let the other team pile on top of them. But they didn't. They pressed on to the

---

9. Acts 14:22, NKJV.
10. Jeremiah 38:6.
11. See 1 Kings 18:17, NKJV.
12. See 2 Chronicles 24:20, 21.

finish line. They honored God. Their Y. A. C. yards call out encouragement to us today!

What firing squad are you facing? Which burly linebacker is plowing into you? You might be trying to solve marital problems. Perhaps your convictions have put you at odds with your relatives. Maybe your lifestyle rubs your neighbors the wrong way. Possibly, you don't fit in at your place of employment because you don't watch the same movies, laugh at the same jokes, or live your life the way your coworkers do. Maybe you're the latest victim of the gossip chain. There are countless ways we get hit.

Don't be surprised and don't be discouraged. God is no respecter of persons. Don't expect Him to spare you from suffering, trial, and unfairness. It's part of the journey. Why? Because this world is the battleground between Christ and Satan. Satan has claimed this earth as his lawful territory, and he takes notice of those who surrender ground to his archenemy, Christ. Anyone who brings honor to Christ and vindicates His character becomes Satan's target, and he works through anyone he can to take them down. It helps to remember that when we are attacked. It helps to see the *mastermind* behind the human agent. He's the real enemy.

But nothing can happen to us without it first going through the throne of grace. Sure, our enemies mean it for evil, but God means it for good.[13] Victory follows a battle, and triumph follows trial.

Stay on the wall!

God said to Nehemiah, "It's up to you, Nehemiah. My honor is at stake. Don't stop until the walls of Jerusalem are rebuilt."

Nehemiah looked at the opposition, the obstacles, and the difficulties. They appeared intimidating, all right. He examined his resources for the task at hand. They were a bit questionable. But God had said, "Run, Nehemiah, run." So Nehemiah ran, and God opened the way.

Endorsed and equipped by the king of Persia, Nehemiah set out for Jerusalem. Knowing that bitter and determined enemies stood ready to oppose him, he planned his moves carefully. Appealing to the hearts of his fellow Israelites, he solicited and gained their cooperation. His hope,

---

13. See Romans 8:28.

his energy, his enthusiasm, his determination were contagious. The people united with him and set their hands to build the walls.

As they crossed the line of scrimmage, the first linemen plowed into them. Sanballat and Tobiah, Samaritan neighbors, mingled with the workers and made fun of them.

"What do these feeble Jews?" exclaimed Sanballat mockingly. "Will they fortify themselves? . . . Will they revive the stones out of the heaps of the rubbish which are burned?"

Tobiah, still more contemptuous, added, "Even that which they build, if a fox go up, he shall even break down their stone wall."[14]

The builders were soon tackled with more aggressive tactics. Adversaries, pretending to be friends, mingled among them, suggesting doubts and causing confusion. They formed conspiracies to entangle Nehemiah and distract him from supervising and encouraging the workers. They spread lies that Nehemiah was plotting against the Persian king.

But Nehemiah continued to look to God for guidance and support, and the people were willing to work. The enterprise went forward until the gaps were filled and the entire wall built up to half its intended height.[15]

Now they hit the third line of defense. Their Y. A. C. yards were mounting! Not only were the Samaritans plotting a warlike attack against Nehemiah and his work, but also some of the leading men among the Jews became disenchanted and tried to discourage Nehemiah saying, "Everyone is tired. They all need a break. There is still so much rubbish to be moved. Let's just give it up." Added to those assaults was another. The Jews living nearby, who were taking no part in the work, gathered up the statements and reports of their enemies and rehearsed them at length to those who were taking part in the work—emphasizing the difficulties of the work and urging that it be stopped.

But taunts and ridicule, opposition and threats, seemed only to stir Nehemiah with firmer determination. He just wouldn't be stopped. His eyes were on His God and His work, and he was immoveable! "We made our prayer unto our God," he declares, "and set a watch against them day and night."[16] He organized the people into shifts. They kept their weapons near at hand while they worked and alternated between

14. Nehemiah 4:2, 3.
15. See Verse 6.
16. Verse 9.

working and guarding so that the work on the wall was always going forward, and watchmen were always poised to sound the alarm if an enemy was sighted.

Seeing that gossip and frontal attacks availed nothing, Sanballat and Tobiah pretended to desire a compromise between themselves and Nehemiah. They invited him to a conference, where they planned to kill him. Nehemiah, however, enlightened by the Holy Spirit, dodged the meeting.

Sanballat then circulated a letter stating that Nehemiah planned treason against the king of Persia, but Nehemiah retorted, "There are no such things done as thou sayest, but thou feignest them out of thine own heart."[17]

Then the Samaritans hired a man that Nehemiah thought was a friend to shut himself up in a chamber near the sanctuary as if his life were in danger. Professing great concern for Nehemiah's safety, Shemaiah advised him to seek shelter in the temple. "Let us meet together in the house of God, within the temple, and let us shut the doors of the temple: for they will come to slay thee; yea, in the night will they come to slay thee."

Nehemiah was not long in penetrating the true character and object of his counselor. "I perceived that God had not sent him," he says, "but that he pronounced this prophecy against me: for Tobiah and Sanballat had hired him. Therefore was he hired, that I should be afraid, and do so, and sin, and that they might have matter for an evil report, that they might reproach me."[18]

The infamous counsel given by Shemaiah was repeated by more than one man of high reputation, who, while professing to be Nehemiah's friend, was secretly in league with his enemies. But their snares failed. Nehemiah's fearless answer was, "Should such a man as I flee? and who is there, that, being as I am, would go into the temple to save his life? I will not go in."[19]

Regardless of the threats, the intimidations, the distractions that his enemies could hit him with, Nehemiah kept his eyes on the goal and

---

17. Nehemiah 6:8.
18. Nehemiah 6:10–13.
19. Verse 11.

kept moving toward it until the wall was finished within less than two months of his arrival.[20] Touchdown!

What is the wall that God has asked you to build? Are you keeping your focus there? Are there any "Samaritans" trying to distract you or intimidate you? Notice that Nehemiah didn't stop building the wall to appease the Samaritans. Neither did he wait for a more convenient time to urge the workers on. He recognized the predetermined hearts for what they were, made appropriate adjustments to his program, and moved on to make a touchdown. His Y. A. C. yards are impressive.

Unfair!

Let's consider Paul again. He and Silas were in Philippi. Through them, a demon-possessed slave girl had found freedom from Satan and thereby deprived her owners of the income they had gained through her soothsaying. Alarmed at the economic implications the gospel might have on their city, they raised an uproar and accused Paul and Silas of exceedingly troubling the city, teaching customs that are not lawful.[21] Then the multitude rose up against them and the magistrates commanded them to be beaten with rods. "When they laid many stripes on them, they threw them into . . . the inner prison and fastened their feet in the stocks."[22]

How unfair! But it happens all the time! It happens whenever we take the gospel seriously and begin to apply it to the work God has given us to do—whether that is repairing a messed-up marriage, redeeming wayward children, or liberating a lost soul. The defense takes notice and makes plans to hedge up our way. Our opponents beat us up—maybe not with literal rods, but with false accusations, with gossip and innuendos. They lay stripes on us—not with literal whips, but with half-truths and rumors that assassinate our characters, our families, or our work. They lock us in an inner prison—not literally perhaps, but by cutting us out of the group or positions or promotions. We're locked out and left to ourselves. We're excluded, banished, and forlorn. Then there are the stocks—those maneuverings to keep us in solitary confine-

---

20. See Verse 15.
21. See Acts 16:20, 21.
22. Verses 23, 24, NKJV.

ment. They tie us up, hold us at a standstill, hindering our ministry, hindering our work. Why? Because we honestly have a different perspective from theirs.

So, how are you doing right now? Have you experienced—or are you experiencing—frenemy fire? When they have you down, beaten, lying on your back, imprisoned with nowhere to go, what is your demeanor? What is your attitude? Are you ready to capitulate? Do you feel a strong impulse to run and hide? Do you long to get revenge? Or will you simply face it?

How do you face it when they have you locked up in a prison, flat on your back, and secured with stocks? There's only one way—and that is with the Spirit of the living God and His Word that promises, " 'I will never leave you nor forsake you.' "[23] " 'I am with you always.' "[24] God didn't forsake Daniel in the lions' den. He didn't forsake Shadrach, Meshach, and Abednego in the fiery furnace. He didn't forsake Paul and Silas in the Philippian dungeon. Neither will He forsake you—no, never!

What a team!

At the line of scrimmage, I observed with trepidation the opposing team lined up shoulder to shoulder, leaving no way for me to get through. They all looked bigger than me! I could see no opening! It appeared hopeless! I might as well have given up at that point!

Then I glanced around at my team. They were lined up shoulder to shoulder between me and the defense. The fullback was prepared to run with me. The right halfback was preparing to cut ahead to make a hole for me to get through.

The quarterback called the play, passed the ball to me, and I started running. But I wasn't running alone! The tight end ran with me all the way, blocking hits at every turn. A huge middle linebacker headed right for me, and I knew he was going to take me down. But before he got to me, the guard blocked him, and I zipped on by. The guy that grabbed my jersey caused me to spin around, but didn't take me down because another of my teammates blocked him and took him out of the play.

23. Hebrews 13:5, NKJV.
24. Matthew 28:20, NKJV.

Nothing touched me without coming through my team first! I was not alone! I built up yards after contact because I was not alone! I made it to the end zone because of the team that was with me all the way!

Do you get the application? Neither will you make it to your end zone without a team. God wants to be your Coach. Jesus wants to run by your side. The Holy Spirit and the heavenly angels are making a hole in the defense's line so that you can go forward. Nothing can touch you without coming through them first. And nothing gets through to you that they can't turn to a good purpose. Without them, you'll never make it. With them, you can't fail! They are there to see that you make a touchdown!

So run! Run in His strength! Run by His side. Run at His instructions! Don't stop until you have finished the work He has given you to do! Don't quit until He calls you to! Don't fail or become discouraged! It doesn't matter how many times you get hit or how hard you get hit or even how many times you find yourself on the ground. That's where the football analogy falls short. Falling to the ground may end the play in football, but not in life. God isn't counting how many times you go down. He's cheering for how many times you get back up!

What an attitude!

That's how Paul and Silas faced the opposing team! They saw the unseen reality of God's heavenly team. They lived in that reality. They knew that the religionists who were out to take them down were no match for the team that ran along beside them. Paul remarks, "In him we live, and move, and have our being."[25]

Picture them now. At midnight, Paul and Silas still lay in that cold, dark dungeon. By now, the blood from their stripes had congealed to what was left of their clothing. The chill of the stones they lay on soaked up through their aching bones, intensifying the discomfort. The position that the stocks forced them into was agonizing. Sleep was impossible. To the hungry, thirsty, exhausted disciples, the opposing team looked invincible. I would have been tempted with discouragement, wouldn't you? I would have been tempted to try to just survive the night and hope for a break in the morning, wouldn't you? I would have

---

25. Acts 17:28.

been tempted to offer up my prayers in silence and self-pity, wouldn't you?

But Paul and Silas caught sight of more than just the defense, didn't they? They looked around at their own formidable Team with the eyes of faith. They focused on their end zone. They counted on a touchdown! They ran their yards after contact in the only way they could right then. They started a praise service! And not a quiet one either!

The other prisoners and the jailer were used to hearing cursing and swearing echoing out of that inner prison, but now they heard praying and singing! They hardly knew what to make of it! Can't you hear Paul and Silas? I can! What depth, what resolution, what focus! They were like Nehemiah refusing to come down off the wall—refusing to give in or give up. What determination! What a legacy of connection to the inward walk. This is a faith that vows, "No matter what, I will praise my God!" It's the loyalty of Job that affirms, " 'Though He slay me, yet will I trust Him.' "[26] That's what frenemy fire does if you let it. It burns the dross and purifies the gold of our characters.

Are you facing a firing squad right now? Are your opponents presenting an invincible line of defense? Do you see no way through? Look a little nearer to yourself. You've got your own Team, and They are ready to run the race with you. Instead of being preoccupied with the moves of the defense, focus on your own Y. A. C. yards. "What play next, Lord?" "Which direction, now?" Don't stop! Keep going!

If you get tackled and find yourself on the ground, don't despair. Sometimes we need to feel our wounds before we feel our need of the Physician. When we open up our wounds to God, He can bring us His healing power, power to live above the slights and slanders of our frenemies, power to go about building the walls instead of engaging our Samaritans, power to sing and pray so that all the other prisoners of the flesh may know the power of the gospel to go beyond religion to the depth of a real walk with God—the God who enables us to sing when we feel like cursing, the God who empowers us to pray when we want revenge and blood.

Frenemy fire—who wants it? None of us do! Who needs it? We all do! We all tend to plateau in mediocrity unless we're motivated to strive

---

26. Job 13:15, NKJV.

for excellence. We all tend to be blind to our deficiencies unless we're made to see them. We all tend to remain spiritual weaklings unless we're stimulated to exercise our faith. Frenemy fire is not just about surviving. It's about thriving!

CHAPTER 10

Y. A. C. YARDS

Questions to Consider for Personal Inventory or Group Discussions

1. When you are hit, do you keep on going, or do you wallow in self-pity?
2. Are your eyes and focus on the end zone (Jesus and heaven) or on those who are trying to take you down?
3. Do you buckle under overwhelming odds?
4. Are you just surviving, or do you thrive?
5. Is your focus to exonerate yourself or to finish the work God has called you to do?
6. Do you allow the circumstances that press you down into despair to become the vehicle for your success?
7. Can you say, "That was the best possible thing that ever happened to me in the worst possible way"?
8. When opposed, do you withdraw, or do you shake the dust off your feet and move forward?
9. How do your Y. A. C. yards stack up against Paul's?
10. Do you expect God to spare you from suffering, trial, and unfairness?
11. Do you realize that nothing can happen to you without it first going through the throne of grace?
12. When God says, "Run," do you run, halt, or retreat?
13. What is the wall God has asked you to build? Are you keeping your focus there?
14. What is your attitude?
15. Do you long for revenge?
16. Do you see that frenemy fire is not just about surviving—it's about thriving?

Keep About Your Work

The Lord has given to every man his work.
It is his business to do it, and the devil's business to hinder him if he can.
So sure as God has given you a work to do, Satan will try to hinder you—
He may throw you from it;
He may present other things more promising;
He may allure you with worldly prospects;
He may assault you with slander;
Torment you with false accusations;
Set you to work defending your character;
Employ pious persons to lie about you and excellent men to slander you;
You may have Pilate and Herod, Annas and Caiaphas, all combined against you,
And Judas standing by you ready to sell you for thirty pieces of silver;
And you may wonder why all these things come upon you.
Can you not see that the whole thing is brought about through the craft of the devil
To draw you off from your work and hinder your obedience to God?

Keep about your work—
Do not flinch because the lion roars;
Do not stop to stone the devil's dogs;
Do not fool away your time chasing the devil's rabbits.
Do your work.
Let liars lie; let sectarians quarrel; let corporations resolve; let editors publish;
    let the devil do his worst.